BEING TAKEN IN

BEING TAKEN IN
The Framing Relationship

Sarah Sutton

KARNAC

First published in 2014 by
Karnac Books Ltd
118 Finchley Road
London NW3 5HT

British Library Cataloguing in Publication Data

A C.I.P. for this book is available from the British Library

ISBN-13: 978-1-78220-071-0

Typeset by V Publishing Solutions Pvt Ltd., Chennai, India

Printed in Great Britain

www.karnacbooks.com

CONTENTS

ACKNOWLEDGEMENTS   vii

ABOUT THE AUTHOR   ix

INTRODUCTION   xi

CHAPTER ONE
The framing relationship   1

CHAPTER TWO
Researching psychotherapy   25

CHAPTER THREE
Learning the body language   43

CHAPTER FOUR
Changing minds   105

REFERENCES   125

INDEX   135

ACKNOWLEDGEMENTS

First of all, I am grateful to Dan and his family for allowing me the privilege of sharing in their lives for those years. I would like to thank Maggie Fagan and Moira Keyes, who both taught me a great deal; I was lucky to have them alongside me in the work described in this book. I want to thank Robin Balbernie for his encouragement and insight, and Zelinda Adam for her patient persistence in taking me in when I was determined not to be. Finally, in writing this book as in so much else, I have been glad of the support of Andrew Harrison, who continues to offer new ways of seeing.

ABOUT THE AUTHOR

Sarah Sutton has thirty years' experience of working with children whose early lives have been disturbing. This has led her to understand disturbed behaviour as a way of trying to communicate something that feels impossible to put into words.

Her master's degree from the Tavistock Centre studied implicit communication as expressed in behaviour. It focused on the dynamic interaction between states of mind/feeling in fostered children and those of the workers in the networks around them. Her doctoral research explored the intersubjective process of meaning-making. She has come to see the primary relationship as essentially a framing relationship, setting the template for a world view in which some things are possible, and others not.

She has an independent practice as a child and adolescent psychotherapist: Understanding Children. She teaches on a Tavistock psychoanalytic studies masters programme, and is a director of the Learning Studio. She is currently working on her next book, *Missing People*.

INTRODUCTION

In trying to help children whose early lives have been disturbing, I have learnt that it is not enough to try and offer a better relationship in which neglect or abuse does not happen. Over the years, I have worked with foster carers, adoptive parents, social workers and teachers who are baffled and frustrated by a child's apparent refusal to know a good thing when they see it. Why might this be? There are all sorts of explanations offered, often to do with control, or even omnipotence. It begins to feel to the adults like a choice the child is making, or refusing to make, and it is sometimes experienced as a perverse choice. Neuroscience, however, tells us something different. In this book, I want to look at what neuroscience and child development studies teach us about how minds are wired, and how they can be helped to change, especially when a child's early life has been disturbing.

I learnt much about the problematic nature of being taken in through working with a boy whom I will call Dan, who had been neglected from birth and adopted at four. It became more and more apparent in three years of psychoanalytic psychotherapy together that the relationship did not feel quite real, somehow. It was as if something was being left outside the room, outside the frame of reference for both of us, while something more fabricated went on between us. This is not to say that what was being made between us had no value, but it seemed to leave out something essential for Dan. As the clinical material in Chapter Three illustrates, he would fight quite hard for this essential something not to be brought in, seen and made explicit in therapy sessions. It seemed sometimes to take the form of a dog that had been badly treated. I found it by turns frustrating and baffling; why wouldn't he let me take in the "badly treated dog" part of him?

There may have been many subtle and complicated reasons, possibly to do with loyalty and identity, but I gradually began to understand a bit more about one of them: that he felt it was a trick—even a conspiracy. I think he may have felt that all the adults were in on it, and so he was a lone child, powerless in a desperately frightening world. He helped me understand that it felt to him as though in taking him into time-limited sessions, I had set a time bomb and the badly treated dog, or neglected child, in his mind was not safe with me. Possibly the trick was also felt to be a risk to both of us—the dog may have looked in need of care and then bitten me, made me ill perhaps. It emerged that it was not a cuddly dog, not felt to be acceptable or impressive in any way. To him, our relationship seemed to be at the expense of this dog, which had to be kept outside. At first this seemed to be a price he was willing to pay, but as the work progressed it became more and more evident how angry he was, and how much he hated me for it.

This dynamic raised the question of the conflicting aspects of being taken in, which can mean being offered a home, but can also mean being the subject of a trick, or even being swallowed up. All of these contradictory meanings seemed to be part of Dan's experience of psychotherapy sessions. In his world, the therapy room was a frightening place to be taken into, even though, or perhaps partly because, he may have felt the need for some of its qualities.

In Hopkins' paper about late adoption she explains:

> One of the risks of adopting children in care is that they may perpetuate their deprivation by rejecting the loving care offered them. Clinical experience shows that, when this happens, it can sometimes be possible to facilitate children's attachment to their new parents by involving them in individual therapy. (Hopkins, 2000, p. 335)

She further suggests that the success of psychotherapy depends upon positive developments in one relationship spreading out to relationships with other people, and she points out that we do not yet have a systematic study of when that process might happen and what might facilitate it.

I do not propose such a systematic study here, but I do aim to trace through my work with Dan the therapeutic process that may help a child with disturbing early experience develop new connections and a different template for relating, thus opening the way towards better relationships in the outside world. In tracing this process, I will use evidence from child development studies and neuroscience of how our template for relating is established in infancy, and look at parallels with the process of psychoanalytic psychotherapy.

Current neuroscience tells us that the intersubjectivity of the earliest relationship sets a frame of reference for experience; a world view that becomes the way in which we understand what happens to us. It follows that the process of being taken into psychotherapy will be experienced in this way—as part of this world, with its prevailing order being the qualities of the early framing relationship transferred onto the person and room of the therapist. The wisdom of Klein's (1952) concept of transference involving the total situation, along with what we have learnt from recent neuroscience, implies that the child in therapy is showing us not just a relationship but the prevailing order of the world inside his or her mind, by which they experience what happens to them. Furthermore, much of this world view is unconscious—not available to autobiographical awareness having been laid down in procedural body memory in the earliest years of life.

The task of the therapist, like that of the new mother, is to offer a world into which the child can be truly taken, with all his impulses and force of feeling. If the child with disturbing early experience is to feel fully taken in, the therapist paradoxically needs to find a way to include the child's fear of being taken in by the therapist. The challenge is how to do this without triggering panic and flight/fright/fight reactions, and thus reinforcing the wired-in connections. In considering this problem, I will look at important evidence from child development studies and neuroscience about emotional regulation (Siegel, 1999) and attunement (Schore, 2003), along with psychoanalytic ideas about temperature, distance (Meltzer, 1976), and levels of work (Alvarez, 2012).

When we can take these qualities into account, the therapeutic relationship acts as a reframing process so that constellations of new mind-brain connections are made, and a new world of possible ways of relating is co-constructed. In this book, I will look at the way in which the early framing relationship is taken into the world of the therapeutic relationship, so that the therapist can get to know it and make connections with it, without being overwhelmed or limited by it. This new way of seeing is taken in by the child, and becomes a new way of being in relation. The therapist is helped in this task by supervision, which offers another world view, outside but able to contain the world of the therapy. What I am describing is not new, but is a reframing of the process of psychoanalytic psychotherapy in terms of the rationale that neuroscience and child development research offer.

Here I would like to introduce Dan, the boy at the heart of this book, who courageously engaged with me on our lengthy journey together, encountering the dilemma of being taken in, and venturing towards possible new meanings in the world of our relationship.

Before I met Dan, I was invited to meet with his parents and other adults in his network to think about what might be helpful for him. As we sat in the meeting room talking, suddenly a slight, spirited nine-year-old boy flung the door open. It was Dan. He had been playing football in the playground while we met, and came in to say that he had lost his ball. He peered curiously round the door at me and ran out again. At this very first meeting, then, there was already a question about whether he should be in the room.

Dan's background was one of severe neglect. He and his brothers and sisters were passed around in the family, sometimes separately, sometimes together, until at three, Dan was taken into foster care. Reports of contact visits at this time portray an undernourished but smiley little boy, eager to please in the face of relative detachment on the part of the adults, who were themselves struggling with a number of difficulties. He was in foster care for a year before being placed for adoption with a family of a mother, a father, and an older brother.

The adoptive family began to find his behaviour challenging to the point of unmanageable. He would attack his parents and trash his bedroom repeatedly. He would also hurt himself; pinching and kicking himself and digging his nails into his skin. Later parent work indicated that his adoptive family found this behaviour unintelligible; he had seemed in this state of mind to be another version of himself, which they could not recognise or relate to. They expressed exasperation at the failure of their attempts to influence his behaviour with rewards and sanctions. After a series of interventions from various quarters, interrupted by funding problems, he began a course of long term intensive psychotherapy with me, supported by parent work with a colleague.

I found working with Dan absorbing and challenging. He often evoked the response of an appreciative audience in me, and I was very aware of the huge deficit in his experience of being an object of wonder and delight. He watched me like a hawk as I concentrated on him, enjoying him and his unique imagination. But it was a performance, and I think it meant that he was still left lonely on the stage. I was helped in supervision to think about other less delightful aspects of him that needed to come in from the cold.

The question was, how? I will look later in Chapter Two at the ways in which neuroscience and the science of perception now demonstrate that what we think we see is what we get. I am using the word "get" here to mean take in or understand as well as receive. The question arises, how would it be possible for Dan to take in something he saw as deeply suspect, without the whole process being warped by suspicion? It would make sense to him to protect his vulnerability by leaving it outside the frame of the therapy and present a performance. As we will see in Chapter Three, his performance had vitality and energy, and evoked delight and wonder; but also communicated the feeling that something much darker was being kept out of sight.

The something much darker seemed to relate to his early procedural body memory of neglect and desperate hunger, experienced in his birth family and stored out of conscious awareness. I will look later at how early implicit memory shapes experience, but would like to point out here that for adopted children there are also elements of experience outside explicit awareness in the adoptive family, which involve the feeling of something unacceptable and excluded. It can be the case that the adoptive family world is felt to exclude the world of the birth family, when adoptive families understandably wish to distance themselves from it in their desire to offer something new, something better. This adds a further layer of complication to the experience of being taken in for the adopted child. It can cause maddening confusion for the child, not knowing to which world they belong, and thus having conflicting ways of understanding what happens to them. Rather than floundering in the maddening confusion this entails, the child, especially when late-adopted, can resort to using the early world view as a frame of reference, and the adoptive family is seen in the context of that prevailing order. For example, late-adopted children sometimes feel that their adoptive parents have kidnapped them from loving birth parents, in keeping with a view of the world to which the birth parents subscribe. For earlier-adopted children this world view is quite unconscious having been laid down in procedural memory, and thus is not available to narrative awareness. For all adopted children, though, the world view is unconsciously transferred to the world of the therapeutic relationship, which is experienced by the child in ways consonant with the qualities of the patterns of relating in and between their multiple worlds—variously unpredictable, conflicting, confusing, depriving, neglectful or abusive, and also at times exciting, and even pleasurable.

The problem, then, is that for the neglected, abused and deprived child, their template for relating is adapted to a neglectful, abusive and depriving world, so that this is not just what they expect, it is what they experience—even at times evoke (Henry, 1974; Emanuel, 2002). We will see in Chapter Three how Dan's early template, adapted to adversity, is applied to the present moment. The question is, how can you change if, as we will see in Chapter One, change happens through intersubjective relationship and you experience the mechanism of change, the relationship itself, as suspect—even dangerous?

In this book, I want to investigate the process by which psychoanalytic psychotherapy can effect change when the mind has been configured to experience relating itself as potentially dangerous. I examine this problem in relation to the feeling of being taken in, which seems to crystallise the contradictory nature of the experience. It seems to link to the confusion and fear evident in children with a disorganised attachment, where the caregiver can be, unpredictably, a source of fear as well as good feelings. These conflicting feelings lie at the centre of the question of how new ways of being in relation can be established for children whose early lives have been disturbing.

In Chapter One, I will begin by exploring the idea of how experience is shaped by the frame of reference we bring to it, not only in psychoanalytic psychotherapy but in everyday life. I will briefly mention the viewpoints of modernism and postmodernism, successively zooming out towards the post-postmodern era of the twenty-first century in which we cannot but be aware of the relational perspective and its shaping effect. I will then turn to a consideration of the framing relationship in the context of psychoanalytic psychotherapy.

The idea of the framing relationship lies in the convergence of the world views of child psychotherapy, psychoanalytic theory, child development studies, and neuroscience. I will first look at child psychotherapy, thinking about the formative impact of the relationship with the maternal mind as experienced by adopted and fostered children, representing those with the most disturbing early experience. Second, I will examine aspects of psychoanalytic theory focusing on ideas about the relational development of the mind and the internal world. Third, I will draw on child development studies with a focus on intersubjectivity and the developmental nature of the primary relationship. Finally, I will refer to findings from neuroscience to do with the subjective, experience-dependent nature of perception and memory, and the interrelation of the two hemispheres of the brain.

Music (2010) shows how these distinct fields of study share common ground; each discipline bringing a different perspective to the way in which a child's early relationships set a template for later relating. I would like to look at the implications of this for being taken into a new framework for relating, both in adoption and in psychotherapy. A particular area of interest is the link between how the child is taken in by the mind of the mother and the child's own sense of him or herself, hindering or facilitating a capacity to take in, or not, what is on offer.

In Chapter Two, my aim is to consider the science of the art of psychotherapy and the nature of research in psychotherapy. I address the central question of what the "raw data" of the study of psychotherapy might be, and how best to interrogate it. This means taking into account scientific studies of the way the mind is built and works; for example, studies of perception that suggest that what we take in is limited or framed by what we can realise. Current neuroscience demonstrates how this, in turn, is framed by our experience of mind-shaping relationships early in life and stored in episodic memory, unavailable for narrative awareness—the psychoanalytic unconscious. This has complex implications for the process of clinical research, particularly the study of the meaning-making that goes on in a psychotherapeutic relationship. In working with Dan, I was reflecting on the experiential process as it happened—a kind of reflexive live research into the way in which we were relating. I consider whether objective and subjective stances in this area are mutually reinforcing, rather than mutually exclusive. After all, observation, even scientific observation, is necessarily based on perception, which, as we will see from objective studies is subjectively determined. I point out that there is inevitably a frame of reference that determines what is inside and what is outside the scope of attention, the focus of the research question. I touch on the idea that this frame of reference will inevitably have implicit as well as explicit elements.

In Chapter Three, I describe the experiential exploration of what works in helping a child like Dan begin to be prepared to risk a new connection with me and with others in his life, despite his background of neglect, deprivation, and serial losses. I use clinical material to trace the co-construction of meanings made intersubjectively between the two of us during the therapy, involving recognition of both negative and positive aspects of the feeling of being taken in as they arose. The material demonstrates the complicated cross-currents of Dan's conflicting worlds, communicated chiefly through body language as they arose in sessions, taken in by me as his therapist and reflected upon. My aim is to show how a new world view is built in the therapeutic relationship, in which the worlds of both the birth and adoptive families can cohabit and interrelate; first intersubjectively in the therapeutic relationship, and then eventually intrasubjectively, once taken in, internally in the child's mind. For reasons of confidentiality, I have chosen not to focus on the interrelating of the adoptive family as it emerged in sessions, although this is intrinsically part of the adopted child's complex situation as I have suggested, and would make a fascinating area of study.

Chapter Four offers an overview, discussing the implications for clinical practice of the overlapping theories of mind-building drawn from the disciplines of psychoanalytic psychotherapy, child development studies, and neuroscience. I suggest that the implications for psychotherapy with disturbed children seem to be that a reframing of the old world view is necessary, and is offered through the process of a therapeutic relationship in which early mind/body connections are experientially brought into awareness in the session, and new meanings are co-constructed in the process. I examine the intrinsic problem that the therapeutic relationship is experienced in the child's mind through the connections made in the early template, so that being taken into therapy—for disturbed children—is thus fraught with all the pain and danger of the early situation. I consider what factors in the psychotherapeutic process may have been helpful in facilitating some change in Dan's capacity to feel himself to be fully take-inable, as it were, and thus to make new connections and develop along new pathways. I will try to show how these factors seem to have had to do with the taking in of implicit qualities; ways of being in relation to each other that were more to do with process than content. These seem to have been expressed in communicative musicality (Malloch & Trevarthen, 2010) and a developing mutual emotional regulation, though importantly in dynamic relation with a more explicit overview, so that body language and narrative awareness could find a connection and a way of being in relation that feels real.

For the boy at the heart of this book, and for all the children I have worked with who have had the courage to help me try to understand

CHAPTER ONE

The framing relationship

D arwin, Marx and Freud's reframing of biological, political and psychological science in the nineteenth and early twentieth century put humans in a different relation to the world than that which had long been assumed to hold sway. The shock of these modern ideas seems to have been not so much the shock of the new per se as the shock of the new perspective—the dizzying step outside to see the frame, the set up. Postmodernism, as the aftermath of these ground-breaking ideas, carried with it the aftershock of the shaken world view: this is not the only way of seeing things. Having noticed the frame, postmodernity, we are in a position to play with the frame. There is a realisation that different frames, ways of seeing (Berger, 1972), can apply, and can affect the content. It raises the unsettling suspicion associated with the postmodern that if perspective is all then nothing is of substance. However, the fact of the frame does not necessarily mean that all ways of seeing are equivalent. The evidence of the neuroscience and development studies that follow seems to suggest that the feeling of substance is created by the qualities of the implicit process. Perhaps those of integrity and authenticity are particularly relevant here. But in an era post-postmodernism it seems to me that we do have to do the work of noticing how the frame affects the content. Berger (1972) alerts the viewer of his own television programme to the frame in the hope that they will be sceptical of it. Post-postmodernism, we have to acknowledge that our framing of experience is always provisional and to be understood in a specific context, but always present; dependent on what we bring to the relationship as well as on what the other brings:

> If what it is that exists comes into being for each one of us through its interaction with our brains and minds, the idea that we could have a knowledge of it that was not also an expression of our-selves, and dependent on what we brought to the relationship, is untenable. (McGilchrist, 2009, p. 37)

The neuroscience of the last two decades has made clear how our social nature depends upon the framing relationship, from which we learn to adapt to the social circumstances into which we are born, and so survive. Schore's (2003) work shows how our very minds are adaptive in this way, developed through the particular primary rela-tionship, as emotional experience makes neural connections which, having fired together, wire together. A child's early relationships thus establish through intersubjectivity the brain patterns that make a mind (Balbernie, 2001).

Furthermore, the qualities of these ways of being together are wired in as a template for relating; a frame of reference through which experi-ence is understood. It shapes the world as experienced by the child and makes some things seem possible, and others not. It seems to me that the implications of this for helping children whose early experience has been disturbing are worth examining.

The idea of the framing relationship arises in the convergence of the fields of child psychotherapy, psychoanalytic theory, child devel-opment research, and neuroscience. I will begin by giving the child psychotherapy context, looking at thinking in this field about work with severely disturbed children, particularly the formative impact of the relationship with the maternal mind. Adoption will be a particu-lar focus, representing as it does severe disturbance in early experience compounded by shifting patterns of caregiving, and offering the chance of a new relational frame of reference in the adoptive family, which is often so bewilderingly hard for the adopted child to take up. I will then draw on psychoanalytic theory of the relational development of the mind, especially Bion's ideas about dynamic containment in relation to the growth of mind, Klein's ideas about the internal world, and Winnicott's thinking on the facilitating environment and the development of the self.

My intention is to make explicit the links between emotional experience and awareness, and so I will draw on child development studies of intersubjectivity, looking at the way in which emotional experience is mutually communicated in the mother–infant dyad. Finally, I will consider findings from neuroscience about the relational nature of the way the mind is built and works, focusing on intersubjectivity as the mechanism of mental development, and the processing interrelationship of the two hemispheres of the brain.

Child psychotherapy and the formative impact of the relationship with the maternal mind

Boston and Szur's (1983) work on severely deprived children led the way in using child psychotherapy techniques with children who had endured very painful early experiences without access to a containing maternal mind, and had then been subject to shifting patterns of care. They noted that "all the children, at times, some in more subtle ways than others, made their therapists feel useless, helpless, rejected, abandoned, messed up or cruelly treated—precisely the experiences and feelings which the patients themselves found intolerable or hard to bear" (Boston & Szur, 1983, p. 58).

Marsoni (2006) considers the links between a child's early and ongoing traumatic experience in the context of the absence of a containing mind, and the absence of his capacity to be aware of the trauma, and thus have a perspective on it, rather than be caught up in it. She connects his inability to "process and transform in his mind the concrete memory of what had happened to him" with his fear "that he could be caught in it again any minute" (2006, p. 313).

Using Freud's "unlaid ghost" metaphor (1909b, p. 122) as a frame of reference, Marsoni made sense of the explosive sessions she experienced in working with an adopted boy during the initial year of therapy. She understood his behaviour in this context, feeling that "through these murderous fights Luke was making contact with his past" (2006, p. 314). She was sensitive to the force of his emotions and sensed that her containing response needed to be limited to naming what he was showing her. She used a "grammar of description", not a "grammar of explanation" (Alvarez, 1997, p. 755). Her feeling was that any attempt to explain or interpret the violence would escalate rather than contain it. There seems to be something important here in relation to the process of co-construction of meaning in the therapeutic relationship. If external therapist-led meanings are applied too readily, it seems to reinforce the child's feeling of not having been really taken in to the mind of the therapist and understood. There seems to be a need for a phase where, paradoxically, in order for the child to be taken in, the therapist is taken into the emotional world of the child. This seems to happen through resonance—that is, receiving the force of feeling from the child. I would like to explore this idea further in Alvarez's contribution to the child psychotherapy literature.

Alvarez's experience of work with deprived and abused children has led her to think about the behaviour of disturbed children as communication, rather than as defence. She writes about a boy for whom "some of my interpretations seemed to make him more mad. He complained that I did not know what it was like to be near a light bulb that is going to explode, and he was right—I was not getting the message" (1997, p. 762).

She was influenced by Joseph's (1978) highlighting of disturbed patients' need for the therapist to be willing to feel the feelings evoked by the patient, and furthermore to feel them long enough "to experience the missing part of the patient" or "his or her previously unexamined internal object" (Alvarez, 1997, p. 755). There seemed to be a need to take in, hold and digest the emotional experience of being with such children, painful and disturbing as it is, rather than serve it back to them too quickly in an interpretation, however accurate, of what might be going on. Alvarez attributes her change of approach in this area to being supervised by someone influenced by Bion's (1959) theory of containment. She stresses the distinction between "the grammar of wishes in neurotic patients and the grammar of imperative needs in borderline patients" (Alvarez, 1997, p. 753). This allows for the developmental importance of offering the containment of primitive anxiety that children with disturbing early experiences have not had. It also involves recognition of their struggle to protect themselves from emotional fallout that they cannot process. In terms of neuroscience, it offers a right brain responsive attunement to their unconscious communication of disturbed states of mind, which can eventually be wired in as the template of a processing function.

Hence emotional regulation acts as a transformative influence on mind change.

Canham describes this dynamic in terms of digestion. In writing about work in a children's home, he notes that the lack of it can mean that a child's feelings and expectations from their previous experience "can easily get recreated between the child and a particular worker, or within whole staff teams". He explains that the "dynamic re-enacting of past experiences that have not properly been understood and digested has, for a long time, been one of the key tools used in psychoanalytic psychotherapy" (2006, p. 260).

Thus the reflective process of exploring the child's mind in psycho-therapy involves a dynamic re-enactment, with experiences from the past relived and experienced in the present moment in the hope of being psychically and emotionally digested—that is, taken in and understood so that the possibility of something new becomes available. The mental and emotional digestive system of the therapist needs to be made available to the child in the way that his or her parents' could not. The wisdom of Alvarez's (1997) paper would suggest that if a child's extreme behaviour in a school or children's home is not taken as an emotional communication belonging to the world of his early experience, which the child desperately needs someone to digest, but is instead attributed to the child, this would exacerbate the feeling of not being taken in and urgently reinforce the behaviour. No doubt those of us who work with disturbed children will have witnessed this painful process.

Although adopted children potentially have their new parents to take in their terrors in a way that is hard for staff to manage in a children's home, they face another difficulty. Associated with the prelude to and lifelong process of adoption, there are heavy losses to be mourned on all sides. An aspect of this theme is discussed in Tollemache's (2006) paper on reconciling the differences between expectation and reality in work with adoptive families. She focuses particularly on the hopes and expectations of adoptive parents, and the difficulty of relinquishing these. Adoptive parents—though not of course only adoptive parents—thus have the daunting task of trying to contain powerful emotions for their children, while inevitably sometimes struggling to contain their own.

Although the expectations that adoptive and birth parents alike bring to the task of parenting are often unvoiced and perhaps unconscious, they are crucial to an understanding of the child's situation and behaviour. They are influential from the first weeks and months of life, or indeed of adoption, in shaping children's attitudes and behaviour. Music makes the point that Winnicott's (1964, p. 88) famous dictum "There's no such thing as a baby" reminds us that "we can only ever understand a baby in relation to the minds and behaviours of those around it" (Music, 2010, p. 2). In the light of this insight, I would like to explore the child psychotherapy literature that describes the effects of shifting, abusive and neglectful patterns of care on the child's own capacity for taking in.

Klein suggests that "in unravelling the details of the transference it is essential to think in terms of total situations transferred from the past into the present, as well as of emotions, defences and object relations" (1952, p. 55). Her idea is that the child will bring to therapy expectations about relationships and mental representations of figures from their past, interacting in their mind and charged with the visceral emotions they carried at the time.

Rustin (1999) discusses the complexity of the adopted child's predic-ament when moves have meant the new geographical and emotional territory is lacking meaningful landmarks and connections. She notes that the adoptive child often carries in mind a plethora of figures: birth parents and other family carers, adoptive parents, significant foster car-ers, and social workers. She alerts us to the "area of disorganised expe-rience" (1999, p. 52) in the child's mind, formed when patterns of care have been too transitory to take shape: different adults in the family car-ing for the child in a disorganised way, institutional care with its shift patterns, or the experience of being cared for by a mentally ill parent.

The implication is that this complicated shifting series of placements constitutes an environmental failure, which is experienced by the child as a formative pattern of caregiving, albeit disorganised, frightening, and neglectful. It is not an absence. As Klein emphasised, the absence of something good, say, a feed, is experienced by the infant as the pres-ence of something bad—a hunger pang. This is borne out by Tronick, Adamson, Als, and Brazelton's (1975) "still face" experiments (dis-cussed further in the child development studies section of this chapter) in which a very short absence of responsive emotion on mother's face is seen to be disturbing for babies.

Klein (1930) suggests that when such a bad feeling is experienced there is a need to seek a representative to stand for the badness as a regulation of this emotion. If such a figure is not available to mediate the experience then the fear is overwhelming, and the internal representation carries the dread of the original feeling; it becomes symbolically equated with it in phantasy. Thus the child who has suffered overwhelming fear without the protective function of a parental mind to mediate and regulate it, in Klein's terms, cannot "distinguish between phantasy and reality in terms of the effect on him or herself, and reacts to the representation as if it were the original feared object" (1930, p. 251). Those of us working with very disturbed children will have seen this happen many times. In more everyday terms, the child is so flooded with fear that he or she cannot tell the difference between their own terror and the intentions of the other. Emanuel (2004) has pointed out how primitive responses are then triggered instantaneously by wired-in connections. Thus the antisocial behaviour of a child taken into public care is to be understood in the context of the frightening early experiences in which mind-body connections were made.

In contrast, where a relationship with a parental figure has helped to mediate suffering for a child, the fear is less overwhelming; there can be a representational object that carries some, though not all, of the emotional load. The frightening experience is processed in the parent's mind, and then begins to be understood between parent and child. It is not borne by the child's immature coping strategies alone, and thus is felt to be thinkable and survivable, inside a frame of reference. The experience is then moderated for the child, first in an external relationship, and then once this is internalised, in an intrapsychic relationship that can bear it, as opposed to the child feeling subjected to an onslaught of overwhelming emotion.

If, as for many adopted children, no adult is available at a critical period to be seen as responsible for the terror, as a representative of the external world, then the child seems to be left with the feeling that they must be responsible, and that the terrifying thing is inside them. Much of the child psychotherapy literature on work with severely disturbed children illustrates this process. Perhaps one way of looking at the purpose of child psychotherapy is to view it as an attempt to take compassionate responsibility for the failure of early relationships and consequent terrors.

I will now turn to key ideas in psychoanalytic thinking about the relational development of the mind and the building of the internal world.

Psychoanalytic thinking about the relational development of mind

Bion's ideas about containment provide a useful starting point. He records being struck by something a patient said to him about not being able to take something in. Building on Klein's (1935) insight that Freud's (1917) shadow of the object does not simply fall upon the ego, but moves in and takes its own shape so that internal representations of objects relate to each other in a whole internal world of object relations, he felt that "the statement that something cannot be taken in must not therefore be dismissed as a mere way of speaking" (Bion, 1963, p. 6).

He went on to say that such words did not just represent but actually conveyed to him something of the nature of the emotional experience. He was being given something to contain—a sense of something not being able to be taken in. He developed from this the idea that something in the patient is seeking containment, and is potentially found by the analyst's mind, in a way that is similar to an infant seeking and being found by the mother's mind. He sees this as taking place in extreme form when the baby is distressed or in pain, such that there is a fear of breaking down or falling apart. The mother's response will be decisive in shaping the baby's feeling about whether the world is a safe place or not; whether fear of annihilation can be contained, thought about, and survived or not.

It is important to note that different mothers will of course experience (and so think about and name) feelings in different ways, thus making different connections in a child's mind. When a child screams, his mother may understand this as a cry for help and seek to allay the suffering, soothing the child and saying that it is a bad pain and will get better. When things go well, both partners can be perceived as loving—to others and perhaps to themselves. "In a loving relationship they can be mutually beneficial. A model of this is the mother with her baby; both can grow through the experience of containing and being contained" (Symington, J., & Symington, N. 1996, p. 58). The implication of Bion's containment theory and Klein's internal world is that the child takes in a number of things from this process: not only the soothing, but an internal relationship in which there is the capacity to soothe, and the capacity to be soothed. Importantly, in understanding the pain as not essentially part of the baby but in painful relation to it, the mother helps the child to separate himself from it; hence there may also be taken in the feeling that the pain is bad but it is not the baby himself that is bad. The infant also takes in the experience of things getting better, and thus the feeling that things can get better and annihilation may not lurk round every corner as he may have feared.

Another mother, however, may understand her child's scream as an attack on her and think of the child as being bad. In this case, what the child experiences and internalises is likely to be very different; perhaps more like an unsoothability and a sense of badness. Furthermore, a relationship is internalised in which things cannot get better and instead can get appreciably worse. Being in pain and frightened with no sense that things can get better, with no separation understood between pain, screaming and child, the child is likely to internalise a feeling that he is himself essentially part of the badness. Perhaps here are some of the roots of disturbed children's damaged capacity to take in or be taken in.

Thus the relationship with the mother provides a context, a frame through which experience can be understood. Perhaps sensation cannot be said to be experienced unless it has gone through this framework. The feeling may be of raw sensory onslaught that makes no sense, for the child has no way to bring it into awareness. Bion writes:

> If alpha-function is disturbed and therefore inoperative the sense impressions of which the patient is aware and the emotions which he is experiencing remain unchanged. I shall call them beta-elements. In contrast with the alpha-elements the beta-elements are not felt to be phenomena, but things in themselves. (Bion, 1962, p. 6)

Bion has used the term "beta elements" for these unprocessed sense impressions to differentiate them from the products of "alpha function" in which a mother is able to experience the baby's disturbing feelings without being overly disturbed herself, thereby offering the possibility of surviving awareness of them. One implication of this is that in contrast to a feeling of disconnected "things in themselves" the mother's response serves the vital function of putting things in relation, of making connections.

In the absence of alpha function, Bion (1963) describes how a child's contact with reality in infancy would have been pervaded by a terrifying sense of life-threatening catastrophe. Bion's disturbed patients attempted to get rid of both this sense of catastrophe and also those functions that might let it in. In the service of this impulse, he suggests that the very sense organs themselves, say, eyes and ears, are felt to be projected out in minute fragmentation as "bizarre objects". These fragments are felt to be lodged in outside world objects, which are then attributed with the psychic qualities of their origins; for example, "impregnated with cruelty" (1967, p. 50), and so the outside world objects are then felt to be charged with the terror of annihilation.

The logic of Bion's thinking along with the process of internalisation not just of figures but of relationships (Fairbairn, 1954; Klein, 1957; Greenberg & Mitchell, 1983) would suggest that this framing relationship lays down the form of the child's capacity for bringing sensation into awareness. It will of course influence the awareness of the adult the child grows into. For fostered and adopted children, the experience of containment is likely to have been compromised at best, or damaging. The intergenerational nature of this process will be evident.

Klein (1930) sees a degree of anxiety, which is not overwhelming, as important for normal development, triggering a capacity for symbolisation. In the terms of this book, the primary parental framing relationship is key here. If there is someone there to help mediate frightening experiences, including that of the child's own angry, hating and destructive impulses, anxiety can be tolerated. Klein's "depressive position" (1935) in which the child can bear for good and bad experiences to be felt to come from the same object and not have to be split off and protected against is achieved. Feelings are less extreme, less life and death; the child can bear for the object to be lost without feeling destroyed, and thus can feel sad and mourn what has gone. For Klein, the symbol— thing, word, or thought—represents the lost object. As Bion working in the Kleinian tradition put it: "Sooner or later the 'wanted' breast is felt as an 'idea of a breast missing' and not as a bad breast present" (1962, p. 34).

But this development presupposes the availability of an attentive maternal mind. It is hard to overstate the significance of this function, evolving in the early infant–mother relationship, which can turn the possibility of catastrophe into meaningful events, experienced as occurring within a frame of reference. When the mother's psyche is open to receiving the signs of catastrophe that her baby emits in what Bion has called "maternal reverie" (1970), the baby's unthinkable fear of catastrophe is transformed, and the baby takes in not only the transformed experience but also the function that transforms, developing a feeling of "going-on-being" (Winnicott, 1956, p. 303) that persists through catastrophe.

Thus the mother's experience frames her response to the child, and the child develops inside and in relation to that frame of reference: a womb with a view. The implication of Bion's theory of thinking suggests that there is a parallel with therapy here. It is not so much that the mother or therapist has named a feeling correctly, more that she will more or less sensitively pick up what the child is feeling, and respond to it with an idea of what it might be, thus offering perhaps in therapy, a room with a view. The view is formative, but not absolutely determinate. It offers a perspective, always provisional, and subject to review. The drawback of the word container is that it invokes the idea of something static, and yet the relationship Bion (1963) describes is one of dynamic interchange; a constant reformulation of subtle and changing nuances. As feelings are expressed between the mother and infant, the mother's idea will frame the experience of that feeling, and the child's response will refine and shape her naming of it, and so the relationship will continue to develop along idiosyncratic ways, contributed to by both of them in mutual resonance. A similar process happens in psychoanalytic psychotherapy. This process of movement between incoherence and integration by naming is an idea that has been furthered by other psychoanalytic thinkers more recently; for example, the work of Bollas.

Bollas (1999) suggests that the technique of free association used in psychoanalysis is essentially destructive of the story of what has gone before, opening the self into an uncertain and open-ended future. In writing about the goals of psychoanalysis, he reasserts Freud's "evenly suspended attention" (1912e, p. 116) as the analyst's invitation to the patient's free association. He proposes that:

> The speaking of deep free associations uses the analyst-other as an object exploiting their suspension of the relational perspective to liberating effect as the self finds in such paradoxical intimacy a deep mutual involvement in a process that deconstructs relational possibilities just as it joins two subjectivities in separate worlds of thought. (Bollas, 1999, p. 66)

I would suggest that free association suspends not the relational itself, for there is a "paradoxical intimacy", but the relational frame of reference that has been mis-set by the early framing relationship when it did not sufficiently meet the impulse of the infant. I will shortly turn to the thinking of Winnicott for whom the impulse of the infant is paramount. However, what Bollas describes is a dynamic process, each element influencing the other, through which interaction a truer, that is, a more attuned meaning develops. This idea of an intersubjective process leading to meaning has links with child development research and with neuroscience, which I will elaborate later in this chapter, but I would first like to note that my understanding of Bion's (1959) idea of the containing response involves more of a moving towards understanding than a total grasp of it. The idea that this relationship is not static but dynamic, that there is an interrelation between the container and what is contained, has implications for the study of interpersonal experience. He sees the element seeking containment as inchoate, unformed, given shape by the receiving container/mind. The implication is that the shape it is given is one of a number of potential forms it might take— the relationship between the two elements influences the form. It provides a frame of reference, or rather, an ongoing framing relationship, without which experience is meaningless.

Applying Klein's theory of the internal world (1958) to this thinking gives rise to the idea that the child will take in not only the content of any one particular example of this process of attributing meaning, but the nature and qualities of the process itself—what the containing relationship feels like. There are studies of the therapeutic process (see Horvath, 2005, for a review) that bear this out, showing that here, too, it is the qualities of the relationship that are most significant in influencing change.

Bion extends his theory to encompass thinking, suggesting that the meeting and interaction of container and contained is how mental growth occurs at every stage of development (Bion, 1970). He suggests that it is possible to see these dual components in the relationship not just between people, but between thoughts. He described this interaction in terms of an impulse seeking a mind to contain it (Bion, 1979). These ideas have a parallel in Winnicott's thinking about holding and the facilitating environment. He saw the facilitating environment as something like the climate in which a plant may grow, the seed of which already contains its own potential fulfilment.

In his (1953) paper, *Psychoses and Child Care*, he focuses on the implications for a mis-meeting of the child's impulse and the thinking mind of the mother. In an environment where there is faulty adaptation to the child's needs, environmental impingement, the child must react to this impingement. The sense of self is lost and is regained only by withdrawal and return to isolation. Winnicott's (1960) theory of the true and false self is based on the idea that the mother needs to meet the creative impulse of the infant without imposing an impulse of her own. Doing this leads the child to begin to orientate itself around the mother, rather than the other way around, and develop along compliant lines, creating a brittle false self rather than a resilient true self that can weather life's storms more effectively.

He sees the parents' task as facilitating the emergence of the true self in its full creativity, able to achieve intimacy and to relate in a way that feels real, not staged or manufactured. It depends on "mother and father's early enjoyment of the person they helped to create", and the lack of it risks "a schism in the mind that can go to any depth—at its deepest it is labelled schizophrenia" (Winnicott, 1964, p. 66). He describes a less serious situation where the split does not go as deep as this, and the protective function of the false self allows life to continue, albeit on compromised terms, and in the meantime searches for suitable conditions.

> The true self is, however, acknowledged as a potential and is allowed a secret life. Here is the clearest example of clinical illness as an organisation with a positive aim, the preservation of the individual in spite of abnormal environmental conditions. This is an extension of the psychoanalytic concept of the value of symptoms to the sick person. (Winnicott, 1960, p. 143)

Perhaps this is a place where psychotherapy may be of value, and the use to which the psychotherapist is put is to seek out and offer a more sensitive response to the patient's feeling. In working with Dan it became apparent that he had developed a false self conveyed by material involving a show; for example, a dancing waiter performance. He had not had much experience of his birth parents' early enjoyment of him, and Winnicott's schism between the dancing waiter and his true self was so deep that it was hard for him at first to use my attempts to put words to his feelings. These attempts seemed in fact to shatter the protective shield of his act and leave him feeling exposed and in extreme danger.

Winnicott's idea of the growth of the true self, then, is that it is already there in essence, and either cloaked in a false compliant self or brought forth to shine by loving parenting. Both Bion and Winnicott's idea is that truth is unknowable, even about oneself. For Bion, versions of the truth are always provisional and to be sought in dialogue between minds or between parts of a mind.

Having looked at some central psychoanalytic ideas about being taken in, to do with the internal world, containment and the facilitating environment, I would now like to turn to the child development studies that bear out these theories and illustrate the crucial importance of the mother's capacity to take in her child's state of mind.

Child development research into intersubjectivity

There have been many studies of the effects of parental attitudes on their children, including, for example, studies of obesity (Johannsen, D. L., Johannsen, N. M., & Specker, 2006), alcohol problems (Jacob & Johnson, 2007), and education (Gorman, 1998). There is not space here to review them all, but they collectively point to the significance of the relationship with parents as a shaping factor in children's lives and behaviour.

Alongside those focusing on problematic areas, there have been a number of studies of factors promoting well-being and resilience in children: parental warmth (Smith & Prior, 1995); the child's perception of parental warmth (Quamma & Greenberg, 1994); emotionally responsive and competent parenting (Wyman, Cowen, Work, Hoyt-Myers, Magnus, & Fagan, 1999); attachment security (Anan & Barnett, 1999; Suess, Grossman, & Sroufe, 1992); resilience (Stein, Fonagy, Ferguson, & Wisman, 2000) and maternal reflective function (Fonagy, Steele, M., Steele, H., Higgitt, & Target, 1994).

For good or ill, then, our earliest relationships shape our lives. This may seem self-evident. However, it is becoming clearer from recent studies of mother/infant relating that these relationships also shape our minds. Research into early infancy confirms the presence of a pre-disposition not only to relate to but to be moulded neurologically by a "virtual other" (Braten, 1988). Braten (2008) explains that:

> Recent infancy research findings, revealing the capacity for intersubjective attunement from birth, have replaced earlier

theoretical views of infants as a-social and ego-centric with a new understanding of infant capacity for interpersonal communion and learning by other-centred participation. (Braten, 2008, p. 134)

He goes on to distinguish three stages in the process from attunement to the internalisation of relationships. The first is primary intersubjective attunement, seen from the very beginning of life and involving body and mind. There is turn-taking and mutual mirroring, with physical gestures mutually reflected; for example, the opening of the carer's mouth in offering food. Secondary intersubjective attunement follows, which introduces a third into the "conversation"; for example, a joint point of interest. Then there is a move towards tertiary intersubjective understanding, emerging in conversational and narrative speech, entailing not only a sense of narrative self (Stern, 2003) and other, but also another level of understanding of others' minds and emotion. This opens the way for emotional absorption, even in fictional others (Harris, 1998), and for seeing things from another point of view, and trying to imagine what might be going on in someone else's mind. Braten's work suggests that this simulation of mind is predicated upon a mutually attuned relationship that has been taken in, and, furthermore, wired in, with neuronal connections established in the developing mind of the baby.

Trevarthen's (1993) work with mother–infant dyads helped establish the basis for these ideas. He argues for innate intersubjectivity as the basis for infant psychology. The mutual resonance between infant and mother when things go well allows for the regulation of positive affect brain states. Gerhardt (2004) describes the importance of sensitive, available care-giving adapted to the baby's needs, along Winnicottian lines. She makes clear the biochemical potential for problematic development when this does not occur; for example, an early overload of the stress hormone cortisol, which effectively sets the stress response in the infant brain to red alert. This has implications for understanding children diagnosed with attention deficit hyperactivity disorder; it would seem that early experience has triggered hyper alert stress responses without an available caregiver's mediating influence.

There have been a number of studies of the effect of an impaired or absent parental state of mind on infants. One striking example that shows how quickly effects take place is the "still face" experiment. Tronick, Adamson, Als, and Brazelton (1975) describe how an infant rapidly grows wary during only three minutes of interaction with a mother looking blankly back. Having made repeated failed attempts to get the interaction into its usual reciprocal pattern, the infant withdraws, and furthermore squirms in evident distress, turning face and body away from his mother, and looking withdrawn and hopeless.

The children in the study showed confusion and distress almost immediately, so tuned in were they to their mother's moods. They soon protected themselves by turning away. This response in the babies showed that even a very brief absence had an effect; a blank face was not neutral for these babies, but seemed to be experienced as something hard to tolerate, which caused distress and necessitated turning away. They seemed to try harder for a while to reach out in order to re-establish normal responsiveness, but then seemed to lose faith in their capacity to enliven their mother's face, and fall apart, almost as if in despair.

The logic of Bion's (1959) theory of the reciprocality of containment would suggest that the experience of unresponsiveness is taken in as part of the framing relationship. It is not the mother's silence that disturbs the babies; it is her lack of response. Thus, it may not be so much the content, a still face, as the process, a lack of mutual responsiveness, which is taken in. The experiment suggests that it is not neutral to be neutral in human interaction, which would seem to have implications for the process of psychotherapy. A blank face, on the evidence of this research, is experienced as disturbing to the infant self.

This may be the case for babies of mothers with depression. A large body of literature documents the adverse effects of maternal depression on the functioning and development of offspring. For example, Goodman and Gotlib (1999) identified maternal depression among risk factors for abnormal development and psychopathology in children. Other research (Field et al., 1988) found that the depressed behaviour of infants with depressed mothers generalised to interactions with non-depressed adults, as early as three months of age. The implication of this seems to be that the relationship with the mother frames all the baby's interactions, not just those with his or her mother. However, there was a hopeful sign in a later study (Pelaez-Nogueras, Field, Cigales, Gonzalez, & Clasky, 1994), which showed that in interaction with familiar non-depressed adults the researchers noticed strong reciprocal influences and the babies' mood lifted. Thus the babies' behaviour was relational; it was to be understood in the context of a particular relationship.

Furthermore, child development studies have shown that our sense of self is laid down in these early years, patterned by our earliest relationships. Stern (1985) describes how abuse or trauma suffered during sensitive periods will adversely affect the nature of this sense of self. He describes the "core self" as being established in babies as young as two to nine months in "not only the feeling experienced but also the experience of interpersonal evocation or regulation or sharing" (Stern, 1985, p. 205). In effect, he is saying not just what is shared between mother and child, but, even more significantly, how the baby is regulated emotionally in their interactions is internalised as not only a way of being but as the core sense of self. Importantly, the qualities of the process of relating are as significant as the content.

For adopted children, this core sense of themselves has had to incorporate painful things. There may have been abuse and neglect, as well as the reality of loss and of having been lost or given away. This seems to be a central point: if the qualities of the framing relationship with the mother establish a core sense of self, then this function being damaged is internalised too, and contributes to the child's sense of a damaged self.

It is hard to see how Winnicott's (1960) true self could somehow be protected from the damaging relationship if the sense of self derives from that relationship. Put in terms of child development studies, attachment is internalised, "being built into the nervous system, in the course and as a result of the infant's experience of his transactions with the mother" (Ainsworth, 1967, p. 429). There would have to be another world in the child's mind, built from other kinds of experience in relating so that other views of himself were possible, and, from what we have seen, this would be formed in relationship. It would therefore necessitate another relationship, with very different qualities. It may be that other family members are important here. It may also be that the framing relationship is a constellation of emotional responses, which includes other qualities than that of damage, so that the sense of self is more multifaceted and complex, and less of a single entity than it sounds. These questions seem to me to merit further study. However, what is clear from this child development research is that the early relationship lays the groundwork for our sense of self—for good or ill, and for our future relating.

Interestingly, the effects of the maternal state of mind have been found to apply to adoptive mothers too, thus overlaying with another layer of complexity the patterns of care that adopted children are likely to have in mind. A study of attachment representations over the first year of adoption (Hodges, Steele, Hillman, Henderson, & Kaniuk, 2003) warrants a closer look, being especially pertinent to the theme of the complexity of the framing relationship for the serially disturbed child.

The study compares adult attachment interviews obtained from adoptive mothers with emotional themes appearing in the play narratives of their recently adopted children—all of whom had been subject to neglect and abuse in their birth families. The authors point out that the more children had been moved from one family to another, the greater the chances they would be highly attuned to the parent figures' state of mind and have an attachment system that is very quickly activated. They reasoned that this might have a kind of survival function, helping them in grounding themselves and trying to understand something of the new emotional, cultural and physical environment in which they found themselves. (See Balbernie, 2010, for a re-consideration of the nature and function of reactive attachment disorder as a survival strategy rather than a mental health problem.) The evidence of the attachment representation research was that themes of catastrophic fantasies, death, aggression, throwing away and bizarre content were significantly more likely to appear in the story completions of children adopted by insecure mothers as opposed to secure ones. It would seem then that adopted children tend to tune quickly into the adoptive mother's state of mind, which acts in a formative way on their own state of mind, and on their world view and expectation of what is likely to happen in life.

There have been other studies of intergenerational transmission of attachment patterns (Fraiberg, Adelson, & Shapiro, 1975; Van IJzendoorn, 1995) focusing on genetically linked parents and children. If we are geared to relate to our pattern of care, which provides a template or frame of reference for understanding experience, there are serious implications for adopted children deprived of an enduring attachment relationship with their biological caregiver, and then undergoing shifts of caregivers.

Alongside the adoptive mother's pattern of care, the shifting caregiving pattern experienced by fostered and adopted children itself is formative, as Rustin (1999) has pointed out. Hodges, Steele, Hillman, Henderson, and Kaniuk (2005) found that late-adopted children with discontinuities of care and multiple placements tested two years into their adoption showed no decrease in negative representations of adult behaviour as aggressive or rejecting. There were some positive changes, for example, in representations of adults as more available and limit-setting, but these did not seem to transform the representations already established.

Furthermore, Bowlby (1980) showed how these various representa-tions form multiple models in the child's mind that require more psy-chic energy than a singular well-functioning internal world made up of coherent representations, and often occur in a context of confusion and fear. It would seem likely that for children who have not only suffered the loss of their primary caregiver, but for whom this same caregiver was often but not always a perpetrator of abuse or neglect, this shifting pattern in a context of confusion and fear may itself become the frame of reference.

It is another link between psychoanalytic thinking and neurobiology that attachment results in the development of internal working models, like the representations of adult behaviour in the studies quoted above (Hodges, Steele, Hillman, Henderson, & Kaniuk, 2003; Hodges, Steele, Hillman, Henderson, & Kaniuk, 2005), which impact upon the devel-opment of later relationships. The impact of caregivers' own upbring-ing affects their relationship with their children, adoptive or otherwise. We have seen how insecurely attached adoptive mothers tend to evoke feelings of impending catastrophe in their children. Traumatic, disor-ganised or disoriented attachments in children often involve an adult whose history includes unresolved trauma. More subtle disturbance in the attachment relationship, such as role-reversal or emotional with-drawal, may also result in the development of a traumatic attachment style (Solomon & George, 1999).

The psychoanalytic wisdom that unconscious expectations about relationships are set by our experience of relationships has thus been established as scientifically valid in child development studies such as those quoted above. I will now draw briefly on findings from neuro-science that show how this process happens; how we are wired for and by relationships, especially our earliest.

The neuroscience of mind-building

Over the past two decades, neuroscience has moved us some way towards a fuller grasp of how early experience shapes our brain (Schore,

1994) and our emotional responses (Perry, Pollard, Blakley, Baker, & Vigilante, 1995; Siegel, 2001). Balbernie explains that a baby's emotional environment influences:

> [...] the neuro-biology that is the basis of mind. From the infant's point of view the most vital part of the surrounding world is the emotional connection with his caregiver. It is this that he is geneti-cally pre-programmed to immediately seek out, register and exuberantly respond to. (Balbernie, 2001, p. 237)

It has emerged in recent years that this emotional connection with the caregiver has a home in the neurobiology of the right brain. A body of neurobiological research shows that the right hemisphere, or "right mind" (Ornstein, 1997), which takes precedence in the first three years, is dominant for the perception and expression of non-verbal communi-cations (Blonder, Bowers, & Heilman, 1991; Dimberg & Peterson, 2000; Schore, 1994, 1998). Schore (2001) tells us that although the process of emotional regulation arises early on in the right brain emotional commu-nications within the mother–infant dyad, this process plays an essential role in all later periods of development. The implications for sensitive maternal attunement are clear. Schore's work shows that the capacity to self-regulate emotion, depending upon social context, "emerges out of a history of regulated interactions of a maturing biological organism and an early attuned social environment" (Schore, 2003, p. 259).

Thus the process of communicating and regulating emotion are intrinsically twined, beginning in the mother–infant dyad intersubjec-tively, in mutual emotional resonance between the two people involved, and then continued intrasubjectively in the growing child's mind in a mental representation of the original relationship, involving the original emotional responses. Both the wired-in intrasubjective experience and the process of intersubjective communication as regulation of emotion continue throughout life, though their developmental impact is greatest in our earliest years.

Importantly for the idea of the framing relationship, the implications are that all later relationships occur in the context of this primary rela-tionship. It is the qualities belonging to this relationship that will, as it were, shape the lens through which future relationships are seen. This relationship seems to provide the emotional frame of reference so that other ways of being in relationship are outside awareness. Siegel writes that how "we experience the world, relate to others, and find meaning in life are dependent upon how we have come to regulate our emotions" (1999, p. 245).

We have seen how emotional regulation happens intersubjectively, each partner tuning in to the other's state of mind. Intersubjective emotional regulation, then, is formative—it is a developmental mechanism. This relates to procedural memory, laid down in the body, of not just *what* but *how* things were experienced, their emotional qualities setting the nature and tone of implicit connections. Schore's (2003) work explains how the orbitofrontal system involved in emotion-related learning retains plasticity throughout life. Here we have the potential for change.

In writing about the reconstructive properties of memory processing, Pally describes how what is later remembered is constructed on the spot, together with all the sensory and emotional impressions of the present moment, and is not an exact replica of what happened in the past. "All the neural elements involved in the processing of events … serve as new information to be stored as additional memory traces of the event" (Pally, 1997, p. 1229). These new neural elements include the emotional qualities of the present intersubjective relationship. Thus the psychotherapeutic relationship offers the scope for change, through new patterns of intersubjective emotional regulation opening new neural pathways alongside old connections. However, it is important to note that for abused and deprived children, the emotional qualities of the present intersubjective relationship can include an implicit feeling of danger, even when there are more positive feelings alongside this. There was evidence of this in the work with Dan that I will come to shortly, and I struggled to find a way to bring this implicit feeling of danger into awareness, without destroying the simultaneous implicit experience of new emotional qualities. For example, he used the symbol of a pot that turns into a volcano, which powerfully communicated his fear of eruption. He seemed to be showing me how frighteningly explosive my attempts at containment could feel for him. He taught me that any bringing to awareness needed to happen first and foremost through emotional regulation; we needed to make the road before we could draw the map.

Before leaving this brief review of some of the relevant neuroscience, I would like to link the idea of a frame of reference to the nature of the relationship between right brain and left brain. The importance of the interrelation between the two hemispheres of the brain for emotional processing is a huge subject and I can only very briefly consider it here.

McGilchrist sums up the distinctive contributions of the hemispheres:

> Ultimately, the left hemisphere is the hemisphere of 'what', the right hemisphere, with its preoccupation with context, the relational aspects of experience, emotion and the nuances of expression, could be said to be the hemisphere of 'how'. (2009, p. 71)

He warns against an oversimplification, reminding us that the two halves of the brain share many functions and interrelate continually, but suggests that overall the left hemisphere deals with the explicit and more conscious processing, while the right hemisphere specialises in implicit non-verbal communication.

Both the content and the process have an impact on the child's experience; what is felt to be happening and how it feels are both shaped by the first relationship, and furthermore are mutually influencing. Does the relation between the two hemispheres reflect the early processing of the emotional impact of sensory experience? Could the way in which the more selectively focused left hemisphere (McGilchrist, 2009, p. 39) assesses and looks for pattern in the broad open awareness of the right hemisphere be a means of seeking Joseph's psychic equilibrium (1989), in the way laid down by the primary relationship? Joseph's idea fits with Damasio's (1999) understanding of the brain as primarily for homeostasis—acting as a processing centre to collect and respond to feedback on body states, and maintain constancy in the human organic system. Damasio's (1999) work elucidates the function of emotion as input into the brain from the internal body environment, just as visual or auditory information acts as input to the brain from the external environment. The interrelation of left and right hemispheres would seem to be a way of selecting what to prioritise of all the plethora of sensory and emotional input of everyday life, particularly when under threat. The left brain categorises swiftly, and while under stress conditions the right brain is overwhelmed and freezes, the left brain acts.

However, the speed of reaction offered by the left hemisphere is bought at a cost. In McGilchrist's (2009) terms, it is equipped to serve an emissary rather than a master role, taking instant separate snapshots rather than the whole moving flow of experience into account. It is associated with grasp in both physical and mental senses; the grasping reflex arises in the left brain, as do the functions of speech aimed at getting a message across, as opposed to those aspects of language to do with musicality, tone and expression, which arise in the right brain. The left brain tends to compete and sunder rather than connect, using categories to serve an agenda. The right brain can take in a landscape, but the left brain, with its focus on fixity and labels, takes the map for the land. Where there is danger, the troubleshooting left hemisphere comes into service to protect. When experience has taught you to fear danger around every corner, the left hemisphere will need to close down the risks of the more open awareness of the right, preventing new ways of seeing the wider landscape of the world and its possibilities. There seems to me to be a warning here about the risk of oversimplifying mental health problems and solutions in complex situations; the mistake of the left hemisphere is to take labelled categories for the real thing.

Overall in this chapter, I have tried to show how the paths of psychoanalytic psychotherapy, child development research and neuroscience converge in demonstrating how the process of early experience shapes psychobiological development in ways which influence our social responses over the course of our lives. In each of these overlapping disciplines, the process of intersubjectivity is seen as essential in establishing a pattern of emotional regulation that becomes a core sense of self, and a template not only for relating but for understanding experience.

I think these ideas have implications for research into psychotherapy, which I will investigate in Chapter Two. Here, though, in summary, I would like to suggest that the process of psychoanalytic psychotherapy entails the unsettling possibility of a shift in perspective, the dizzying step outside the frame that calls the previous world view into question. Without the signposting that this earlier world view offers, we feel we risk being left, disorientated, in no man's land—with its potential landmines.

However, it would seem on the evidence of the neuroscience we have seen that the emotional qualities of the relationship with the therapist help establish a pattern for new experience. The psychotherapeutic relationship thus itself provides an experiential bridge across no man's land from the old world view to the new, which can then be mapped in left brain ways. The old world can eventually be re-signed, though not removed.

Psychoanalytic psychotherapy is designed to explore the wired-in body memory of troubling relationships in the context of the therapeutic relationship, so that experience is not removed but reframed in a way that feels both real and liveable. McGilchrist's work highlights the need for right brain responses that take left brain triggers into account, bringing to mind the developments in child psychotherapy relating to resonance and emotional temperature led by Alvarez's (1993) ideas about how thoughts become thinkable. In this way, the left brain can gradually and gently be relieved of its patrol duties now and then, so that new possibilities can emerge and be considered, and new ways of seeing, thinking and feeling can be made available.

CHAPTER TWO

Researching psychotherapy

The subject of research into psychotherapy is increasingly urgently considered as ways are sought to establish effective professional practice in a world of shrinking resources and expanding demand. There is an emphasis on the need for measures that indicate effective interventions and so attract scarce resources. This is all the more interesting and necessary given the nature of psychoanalytic psychotherapy, explicitly aimed at exploration of unconscious processes and subjective, intersubjective, and intrasubjective connections and meanings. How do you study the process of co-constructing new meanings in relationship and thus rewiring brains that is involved in psychoanalytic psychotherapy? Like the practice of psychoanalytic psychotherapy itself, research into it seems to be situated in the overlap between the worlds of science and art. It seems to me that neuroscience is a useful guide in this area, and indeed Schore's (2012) most recent book is entitled *The Science of the Art of Psychotherapy*; perhaps he might equally have called it the Art of the Science of Psychotherapy.

There are ideas and assumptions about the nature of subjectivity and objectivity, indeed about the nature of research and of scientific enquiry, embedded in the debate about research and outcomes. I would like to consider whether, in the light of recent neuroscience and child development research, it is possible to see objective study and subjective meaning-based explorations not as mutually exclusive, but as mutually reinforcing; each potentially contributing in an integrated way to an understanding of how psychotherapy works. The interaction of the objective with the subjective presents a challenge to traditional research methods, but new ways of approaching research are being found. It has recently been suggested that "psychotherapy research is no longer concerned with efficacy but rather with how effective change occurs" (Tschacher, Schildt, & Sander, 2010, p. 578). I would like next to examine some research into how change happens, and what might constitute the "raw data" of the study of effective change. This will involve looking at notions of objectivity, subjectivity, and intersubjectivity in the research process.

What is the "raw data" of psychotherapy research?

As we have seen in Chapter One, the formation of a child's internal world happens in relation to the internal world of the mother, as a guide to the external world into which the child is born. The psychotherapeutic relationship is also a frame of reference into which the child is taken, and in relation to which they are understood. Essentially, psychoanalytic psychotherapy could be understood as exploring the first of these relationships in the framework of the second.

This book is an attempt to offer the results of such a process for consideration, and, like all research undertaken by psychotherapists into their own practice, it involves a paradox inherent in the notion of interrogating a relationship in which one has oneself participated. Is it possible to be both inside and outside the relationship? There are ideas in psychoanalytic theory about the third position creating triangular space to help facilitate this process. In working with disturbed patients, Britton writes about his own need for "a place in my mind that I could step into sideways from which I could look at things". He found that the only way of doing this that was not disruptive to the patient was to "allow the evolution within myself of my own experience and to articulate this to myself, whilst communicating my understanding of the patient's point of view" (Britton, 1989, p. 92).

This seems to convey more depth than is intrinsic to the two-dimensional triangle. It suggests to me that Britton envisages the world of the patient within the world inside his mind. He can step into the internal world of the patient as conveyed by the material and its emotional qualities, and also step out of it while still containing it in his mind. It is well-established that supervision also helps to create a reflective consideration from another point of view. My work with Dan benefited from supervision in many ways, offering another stage of reframing—another world view.

However, I want to go back a stage and consider ideas about conveying the two-person process as it happens, before there is a chance to reflect on it. Is there a moment before Britton's sideways step that might constitute the raw material, as it were? I think this question is worth considering in relation to the wider notion of research into psychotherapeutic encounters and how effective change occurs.

What we have to go on in discussing a psychoanalytic encounter is an account of what happened in the room, to the best of the knowledge of the person giving the account—in this case, me. The parameters of the raw data may be considered to be boundaried in space and time by the limits of the session room and hour: what happened in the room during the session. However, there is a difficulty in that we do not have access to the entirety of what happened in the room, or even to an objective account of it in all its fullness. Even the most thorough account necessarily makes omissions—for reasons of time and space, but also, importantly, because of not being able to notice everything. After all, even a camera has a point of view, and furthermore, filming someone in a psychotherapy session is not neutral. The account is thus inevitably selective—what happens is seen through the lens of my experience. In effect, the account I give can only serve as a snapshot, more or less reliable depending on the qualities and breadth of my own experience.

As any police person collecting evidence will acknowledge, it is not possible to know absolutely what happened in the room. Different witnesses to an accident or crime give different accounts of what happened, even to the extent of disagreeing about physical details with some impact, like the colour or speed of a car, say. Furthermore, they will be influenced by the point of view of another person. For example, Loftus and Palmer (1974) in their studies of eyewitness testimony found that the way in which questions were framed influenced participants' answers. In assessing the speed at which a car travelled in a short film, participants were twice as likely to report a faster speed if the question used the verb "smashed" rather than "made contact", or asked about broken glass, even though there was no broken glass in the film. The words "smashed" and "broken glass" seem to have suggested a frame of reference involving greater speed, and respondents reported speeds commensurate with the picture evoked in their minds by these words, rather than the picture they saw on film. This suggests to me what social animals we are, and just how mutual is the process of meaning-making; the respondents seem to be consciously or unconsciously looking for common ground with the researcher.

Even very early studies of memory (Bartlett, 1932) demonstrated how memory is not a static storehouse of traces, but instead forms and reforms in dynamic relation to context and schemata of experience. Bartlett described remembering as both a constructive and re-constructive process; relative, not absolute. We might add from the evidence above that it is a co-constructive process. Bartlett also established that awareness is not necessary for memory. It seems that we unconsciously try to fit past events into our existing representations of the world, making the memory more coherent so that it makes more sense for us.

Pally (1997) explains the construction process of memory in wiring-in emotional experience in which "the hippocampus-frontal index joins together the individual sensory features, time and place of the experience" (Pally, 1997, p. 1229), so that emotional, geographical and other aspects are linked together, and potentially triggered later by association.

However, even if we accept the analogy of the relatively neutral albeit selective camera, my question is, is it possible to separate the picture from the camera angle, or from the frame? Bartlett's studies and Pally's research would suggest not. Furthermore, I wonder if the camera angle, or the process akin to a viewfinder window through which we choose and frame the picture to be taken, in which we select from all the plethora of available minutiae *what* to focus on, inevitably affects *how* the child is thought about, and therefore affects the relationship. Putting it the other way round, does *how* we think about a child affect *what* we can think about? I will look later at studies of social attitudes affected by metaphor, which suggest this is so. But here I would like to ask, do we notice the behaviours that make most sense to us in relation to an idea already in our minds, a preconception? There is evidence to suggest that this happens. Typing the phrase "count the basketball passes" into an internet search engine at the time of writing (2013) reveals a brief awareness test that demonstrates how it is surprisingly easy to miss something you are not looking for.

This affects the notion of "raw data". The briefest skim through studies of perception (see Merikle, 1998, for a review) tells us that even the most basic visual perception is shaped by what we "know". For example, where there is light shining on two angled white panels, a light meter would read that one side of the panel is white and that the left side is grey, being more in shadow, yet our visual systems interpret them both as white. Our eyes compensate for ambient lighting, so that under almost all conditions the colours appear stable (Greene, Easton, & LaShell, 2001). Furthermore, visual information overrules auditory input, which the authors of this study describe as providing "constraints on ambiguity" (ibid., p. 425). The idea of constraining ambiguity is interesting, and links with left brain functioning as discussed in Chapter One. Absence of ambiguity is desirable in an unknown environment, with its threat potential. It seems that we have evolved to prioritise safety over new possibilities: better wrong than dead.

Perceptual experience, then, is not just a function of what hits the eye; it is a function of the interrelationship between what comes in from the outside world and the central nervous system. Furthermore, it is interpolated by interrelationships within the brain: interneurons convey messages between the sensory and motor neurons and in fact make up the main body of the brain. The conclusion of a study of conscious and unconscious perception was that "perceptual processing itself is unconscious and automatically proceeds to all levels of analysis and redescription available to the perceiver" (Marcel, 1983, p. 197). Marcel's findings cast Hegelian (1807) doubt on the assumption that there is equivalence between what we see and what is there; it is mediated.

For the purpose of scientific research, this information is central. My microbiologist father sees science as starting with an intuitive premise. In a recent lecture, McGilchrist (2013) suggested that such an intuitive premise would arise from connections in the awareness of the right brain, and the left brain would then be harnessed into action to collect data and report back. The question of what data might be collected goes to the heart of the subject of researching psychotherapy, especially given that we are considering an experiential process. The studies mentioned above would seem to imply that data, whether explicitly experiential or not, can only ever be taken into the mind in a relational way. The question can be expressed in terms of neuroscience: how would it be possible to filter out the "actual" object from what we perceive, if not through the visual systems that interpret in relation to other parts of the brain formed in relation to experience? This phenomenon is the basis for optical and other illusions. We make a best guess based on previous experience and are oblivious to its provisional nature.

The experience we draw on to inform our best guess is often subliminal. In his tricks on the public, for example, the magician Derren Brown makes much use of subliminal suggestion. He is able in subtle but simple ways to influence choices made by his subjects, in ways they themselves are unaware. He has implicitly signalled the behaviour he expects to elicit. For example, the potentially open task of writing an advertising campaign was shaped, in ways that Brown could predict, by the people who conceived it having been driven past specific motifs that were then included in the campaign (Channel 4, 2012). There is reason to suppose that we are influenced in other relationships in similarly implicit ways, especially but not only in our primary early relationships in which we are discovering how the world works and our place in it. In evolutionary terms, this makes sense. Bowlby described how an infant needs to and does adapt to his or her specific social situation through taking in the implicit rules of engagement in an ongoing dynamic process (Bowlby, 1969).

Arguably any study needs to acknowledge, then, that there is no such thing as neutral raw data; that the very act of perceiving is not neutral but happens in relation to expectations drawn from experience, and is revised in memory according to new circumstances. Returning to the study of psychotherapy, it is clear that the relationship itself inevitably frames and shapes the meaning attributed to the encounter. The logical implication is that data offered for consideration would need to include some indication of context as well as content; for example, clinician responses and attitudes as well as those of the child. The Tavistock infant observation model introduced by Bick in 1948 and described further below is one such research model. It records context and observer emotional responses along with external observations, explicitly acknowledging the infant, and indeed the observer, as acting in and acted upon by the context.

Ainsworth and Bell's (1970) work on the "strange situation" also captured the subtleties of dyadic interaction in observational measures that took into account both content and context. It is noteworthy that the context has an effect. This is not necessarily used consciously as it is in advertising, although that field is a substantial body of evidence in favour of the experience of form and content being relational rather than absolute. For example, in Dichter's (1964) experiment, the colour of a coffee can affected participants' experience of the strength of the coffee it held. The same coffee from brown, red, blue and yellow cans was variously experienced by respondents as too strong, richer, milder, and too weak. In another example of the experience-affecting, sense-making properties of cues about context, Pilditch (1973) in his book, *The Silent Salesman*, explained how the picture of a spoon on the packaging of a baking product was an implicit cue that made it possible for the housewife to mentally rehearse the use of the product while it was still on the shelf.

It is interesting to note that long before the days of advertising, and of Marshall McLuhan's (1964) ideas about the medium as the message, Freud was careful to formulate his interest in the workings of the mind in scientific terms. There are signs that Freud's contemporaries, Jung and Ferenczi, wanted to explore the wilder shores of spirituality, and Freud (1911) in private letters seems to have shared their interest. However, what he wrote for public consumption in his (1895a) *Project for a Scientific Psychology* was framed squarely in terms of objectivity, of causes determined by neurophysiology. There may be a parallel with the UK National Institute for Health and Care Excellence project, which seeks to objectify excellent clinical practice in order to spread it more widely, and possibly speed it up. In the attempt, it may be that the effort to be and be seen as "scientific" means that the relational and the emotional are overlooked. The very word "clinical" implies a cool detachment, as if it would need to exclude the emotional, the subjective. However, it is increasingly clear that our neurophysiology is objectively intrinsically relational, and furthermore, that our thinking is predicated on emotion (Damasio, 1999). The worlds of science and emotional relationship are perhaps not as far apart as they seem. Objectifying excellent clinical practice would thus need to involve taking into account the neuroscience of relating, and of right and left brain processing.

The prevailing world view of science has been one in which emphasis is laid on an idea of objectivity involving separation between observer and what is observed, which ironically does not stand up to scientific scrutiny. The philosopher Midgley's review of Sheldrake's (2012) book, *The Science Delusion*, suggests that we "can't go on pretending to believe that our own experience—the source of all our thought—is just an illusion". She laments the "unlucky fact that our current form of mechanistic materialism rests on muddled, outdated notions of matter", and calls for "a new mind-body paradigm" that acknowledges human beings "as the active wholes they are" in order to approach important mind-body topics. Sheldrake's book argues that the scientific world view has become a belief system, with assumptions hardening into dogma. These are qualities we associate with the left brain, which, as we have seen, has excellent categorisation skills, but is on the whole better equipped for defence of the status quo than for exploration.

Framing the discussion

McGilchrist suggests that "conventional neuroscience, being itself largely a manifestation of left hemisphere activity, has focused ... on what the brain is doing in each hemisphere, thus in my view, missing the significance of what it was trying to understand" (2009, p. 93). He questions whether this approach could be read "as the misapplication of language—in other words, the faulty procedure of seeking truth by standing in the world of the left hemisphere while looking at the world of the right" (ibid., p. 89).

The insight that the language we use limits the thinking we can do, and vice versa, lies at the heart of psychoanalytic wisdom, and applies, of course, every bit as much to the discussion of psychoanalytic psychotherapy as it does to any other conversation. The parameters of a discussion are set by the choice of terminology. Thibodeau and Boroditsky's (2011) work on the relationship between language and responses to crime shows how the contrasting use of "virus" and "beast" metaphors for criminal behaviour elicited very different subject responses. They noticed that once even a single word metaphor was introduced people used it as a governing concept and made frame-consistent inferences. Interestingly, they found that the influence of the metaphorical framing effect is covert, working implicitly.

Thus the way in which we describe what happens affects what we think and feel, subliminally. Damasio writes that "an important consequence of the pervasiveness of emotions is that virtually every image, actually perceived or recalled, is accompanied by some reaction from the apparatus of emotion" (Damasio, 1999, p. 58). What he says suggests that it is not possible to separate perception, memory, or thought from emotion. In being scientific, we cannot avoid either the emotional or the relational.

However, there are of course many scientifically validated studies of this interrelation, involving the duality and mutuality of meaning-making. Schore writes powerfully about the paradigm shift in the mental health field, involving an "ongoing dialogue with neighboring disciplines, especially developmental science, biology, and neuroscience" (2009, p. 112). He sees this mutually enriching dialogue between disciplines as centring on a common interest in the primacy of emotion.

Schore's work makes a specific connection between neuroscience and psychotherapy. As I mentioned earlier, he explains that the orbitofrontal system, involved in emotion-related learning, retains plasticity throughout life. This, he writes, "may help us understand how affectively focused psychotherapy can alter early attachment patterns" (Schore, 2003, p. 69). Thus, importantly for effecting change through psychotherapy, it seems that what we take in early in life may be influenced by later relating. He outlines the science of relationship, explaining how relating forms or alters mind and emotion. The neurophysiology of emotion and meaning-making is intrinsically relational, not independent. This has a direct bearing on the theme of this book. Whatever meanings are ascribed by children to their own losses and separations are created in relation to the behaviour of and feelings conveyed by their caregiver(s). Can these meanings made intersubjectively early on, at the core of a child's sense of self, be adapted in the intersubjectivity and emotional regulation of a later relationship? I will try to trace an individual development of this process in Chapter Three, but, importantly, Schore points out that it lies at the heart of the psychotherapeutic endeavour, suggesting that current studies of the unconscious domain not only support a clinical psychoanalytic model of treatment, but can "elucidate the mechanisms that lie at the core of psychoanalysis" (2010, p. 177).

He explains the way in which child and therapist communicate unconsciously alongside conscious explicit attention to what is said and done: "listening and interacting at another level, an experience-near subjective level, one that implicitly processes moment-to-moment socio-emotional information at levels beneath awareness" (Schore, 2010, p. 184). He thus offers the science illuminating the intersubjective process of unconscious communication, in the making and the taking in of meaning available to the patient's implicit sense of self, specially located in the right brain, which is particularly active in psychoanalytic psychotherapy. "Indeed the implicit functions and structures of the right brain represent the inner world described by psychoanalysis since its inception" (Schore, 2010, p. 179).

Earlier, I touched on the evidence for the clinically observable concept of intersubjectivity in child development research; for example, Braten's research confirming the presence of a predisposition to not only relate to but be moulded neurologically by a "virtual other" (Braten, 1988). Trevarthen's work (1993) on intersubjectivity with mother–infant dyads bears this out, and suggests that the mutual resonance between infant and mother allows for the regulation of positive affect brain states. This regulation is transformative. "The baby's brain is not only affected by these transactions, but also its growth literally requires brain-brain interaction and occurs in the context of a positive affective relationship between mother and infant" (Schore, 2003, p. 42). The significance of this for children who have suffered disturbing early relationships is profound. They have not experienced the emotional regulation that facilitates healthy brain development.

Schore elucidates the process by which the infant's right hemisphere, dominant in non-verbal communication, uses the output of the mother's right hemisphere "as a template for the hard-wiring of circuits in his own right cortex that will come to mediate his expanding cognitive-affective capacities to appraise variations in both external and internal information" (2003, p. 44). Thus the mother's state of mind is not only the climate in which the baby's mind develops, it also establishes the navigation system by which the child will steer a course through the world, and watch out for dangers. It establishes the way we see the world in which we live.

Intersubjectivity, then, the mutual resonance and regulation of physical/emotional states, is discovered to be the neurobiological mechanism by which the brain and mind develop. The implications for intersubjectivity as the mechanism of change in psychotherapy are clear. Indeed, Schore's work places this process at the heart of psychotherapeutic effect. He explains that the right brain plays an important part in the process of psychotherapy, its role offering:

> [...] a model of implicit communications within the therapeutic relationship, whereby transference-counter-transference right brain to right brain communications represent interactions of the

patient's unconscious primary process system and the therapist's primary process system. (Schore, 2010, p. 182)

In their work with mother–infant pairs, Beebe and Lachmann (1988) observed a mirroring sequence—synchronous rapid movements and mutually responsive affective expressions happening literally moment by moment or faster. Schore writes that "the fact that the co-ordination of responses is so rapid suggests the existence of a bond of unconscious communication" (2003, p. 38). The existence of a bond of unconscious communication, scientifically validated and bearing on the development of mind and emotional processing, seems to offer a link between the apparently polarised camps of objectivity and subjectivity. Alongside the empirical facts in Schore's painstaking research and comprehensive review (1994), the use of functional Magnetic Resonance Imaging (fMRI) of the brain is perhaps as empirical as it gets in this area.

Importantly, studies using the fMRI technique have found mirror neurons in the human brain that fire in the same region when witnessing an action performed by someone else as when the subject performs the same action. (For an overview, see Rizzolatti & Craighero, 2004.) This suggests that intersubjectivity is not only an emotional and mental process, but bodily based as well; essentially, "limbic resonance based on activated mirror neurons" (Balbernie, 2007, p. 312).

Furthermore, "premotor mirror neuron areas—active during the execution and the observation of an action—previously thought to be involved only in action recognition are actually also involved in understanding the intentions of others" (Iacoboni et al., 2005, p. 1). Hume's (1748) predictive relationship, whereby an effect can be deduced from a cause, is in evidence here. Mirror neurons will fire in someone observing an action—even in anticipation of observing an action—more strongly when there is a clear context for the action witnessed. These child development and neuroscientific studies seem to bear out the view that non-verbal intersubjectivity—unconscious communication— is a scientifically verifiable process, crucial in the development of meaning, which is inferred from the context.

So we have scientific proof of babies learning to process the world and their responses to it through mutual attunement with a caregiver, of the human mind and body prone to feel what another feels on witnessing an action—even on anticipating an intention, and furthermore we have studies of visual perception that suggest that what we see is subjectively determined by what we already know. Barlow writes:

> It is a mistake to consider perception and learning separately because what one learns is strongly constrained by what one perceives, and what one perceives depends on what one has experienced. (1990, p. 1561)

It becomes apparent that processes dependent upon the notion of objectivity, such as scientific research, cannot avoid the subjective, inevitably relying as they do on perception. Meanwhile the significance of subjectivity is objectively supported by an increasing body of evidence, including fMRI scans. Many of the central tenets of psychoanalytic thinking—including the central one of the unconscious itself—have been borne out by the studies I have touched upon, so that the polarity between research framed in terms of objectivity and more subjectively-focused meaning-based studies begins to seem reductive. There is evidence of biological cause and effect in the making of subjective meaning. For example, Schore's work makes the specific connection I have already mentioned between neuroscience and the intersubjective process of psychotherapy. Indeed, Glass states:

> Recent research in brain imaging, molecular biology and neuro-genetics has shown that psychotherapy affects brain function and structure. Such studies have shown that psychotherapy affects regional cerebral blood flow, neurotransmitter metabolism, gene expression, and persistent modifications in synaptic plasticity. (2008, p. 1589)

There has long been a tradition of writing about psychotherapy in terms of metaphor and art. It is increasingly apparent that through the processes of free association, transference and countertransference we have been, perhaps initially unwittingly, doing something scientific: modifying synaptic plasticity in such a way that it persists, wiring in new connections in the brain through the therapeutic relationship.

Woody and Phillips' revision of Freud's *Project for a Scientific Psychology* suggests that it may now be possible "to form a notion of the unconscious that is clinically formulated and neurophysiologically grounded" (1995, p. 123). There is a caveat: in parallel with Ricoeur (1970), they warn against thinking of the psychodynamic unconscious as ruled by linear logic, and suggest that instead there is complexity. They use the analogy of an internal "unruly crowd of interacting meanings" (Woody & Phillips, 1995, p. 123), bringing to mind Adam Phillips' model of the analyst as host, making introductions to the uninvited guests of the patient's unruly or bizarre disowned unconscious (1995, p. xvi).

This view is supported by Wittgenstein's *Philosophical Investigations* (1953) in which he warns against trying to tie meanings down in words, and so make difficulties that do not exist in the course of experience. His wisdom seems to suggest the relation between left and right hemispheres of the brain in which the left brain continually works to find a template, a boundary or an explanation for the right brain's inflow of experience as it is felt in the moment.

My aim here has been to explore the limitations of the view that there is a polarity in research approaches between objectivity and subjective meaning. Indeed, there seems to be a fruitful and fascinating dialogue between the two. Beebe and Lachmann's (1988) mirroring sequence and Schore's (2003, p. 38) bond of unconscious communication show how our physiology works towards making meaning intersubjectively, and this has a parallel with psychoanalysis, and the study of psychoanalysis. We need to use research methods that acknowledge this complexity, and bear witness to the primacy and subtleties of emotion; ways of looking that fit the subject, rather than the other way round. I will now turn to a discussion of approaches that seek to address this need.

The observational approach

> For if you look at them you will not see something that is common to all, but similarities, relationships, and a whole series of them at that. To repeat: don't think, but look! (Wittgenstein, 1953, aphorism 67)

Wittgenstein's injunction not to think but to look seems to prefigure McGilchrist's work on the two hemispheres of the brain, with their very different roles, purposes, and attitudes to knowing. McGilchrist describes the left hemisphere as favouring analytic sequential processing, seeing knowledge as a picture built slowly, piece by piece, out of factual "certainties". The right, on the other hand, he portrays as getting to know through the flow of a relationship, "a back and forth process between itself and other", which "is therefore never finished, never certain" (McGilchrist, 2009, p. 229). He points out a huge disadvantage of this approach to experience: the difficulty of passing it on. A distinction is made between knowing about and knowing, which brings to mind Bion's (1962) ideas about learning from experience.

This problem seems to lie at the heart of the attempt to find ways of writing about psychoanalytic psychotherapy that may give its insights and therapeutic successes social and political currency. However, recent neuroscience and child development research represented by the work of Schore (2012), Siegel (1999), Stern (2004), and others offer a way forward. I have tried to show how in the science of intersubjectivity outlined above it becomes apparent that our psychobiology can objectively be seen to work towards making meaning, intersubjectively, and that effective practice, and research, must therefore take this into account.

In their book, *Researching Beneath the Surface* (2009), Clarke and Hoggett state that traditional models of human rationality, which opposed thought and emotion as "reason and passion", are being challenged. They suggest that "as ways have been sought to overcome such splits, psychoanalysis has increasingly appeared in the breach" (2009, p. 1). They note that psychosocial studies use psychoanalytic concepts and principles to illuminate core issues within the social sciences, and inform the development of new methodologies in that field. These use a number of psychoanalytically grounded interview and observational methods, and attend to interpersonal dynamics in the research process. The attention to interpersonal dynamics, particularly the emotion aroused in the observer, is a cornerstone of psychoanalytic thinking. It is a central feature of infant observation that Bick (1964) pioneered as a method of researching human development to inform training in psychoanalytic practice. Its scope over the years has widened to include many other trainings. "As an observational method that enables access to a reflexive understanding of the observer and the observed, it has much to contribute to the wider field of the social sciences" (Briggs, 2002, p. 280).

Rustin (2002) makes the point that researchers in infant observation are not looking for sequences of linear development, but for "ordering patterns, for the evidence of emergent systemic organization in the minds of infants and in the relationships between infants and those around them" (2002, p. 271). He argues that looking for patterns of relating in this way better fits the complexity of the "self-organizing system" of the human subject than a mechanistic model. He makes a link with complexity theory, suggesting that it pertains to:

> [...] a large domain of nature that is neither determined in the manner of a closed mechanism ... nor wholly random ... Instead, it posits self-organizing systems of high complexity and indeterminacy within understood limits. This domain is precisely ... the world of experience with which clinical psychoanalysts continually struggle and which infant observers encounter. (Rustin, 2002, p. 278)

In a foreword to Urwin and Sternberg's book, *Infant Observation and Research* (2012), Hollway writes of finding in infant observation a research method that:

> [...] put the relationality of the infant and infant's carer(s) at the centre of the paradigm and could preserve the social setting at the heart of the research encounter ... Here was a method that taught a way for observers to cultivate objectivity, not in the positivist sense of the word, but in the sense of paying attention to their emotional responses and noticing when, where and how these informed their understanding of what they were observing. (2012, p. xiv)

The observational method is useful in researching psychotherapy in that it bridges the concepts of objectivity and subjectivity, offering therapist-observed, necessarily subjective, interactions between child and therapist for consideration. An observational approach allows the important resource of the therapist's emotional responses to be used as information about the therapeutic encounter. This method offers scope to make more explicit the process of intersubjective, often implicit, meaning-making in the therapeutic relationship. It allows us to seek Rustin's (2002) "ordering patterns" rather than linear developments, which seem to better fit the complexity of the material under study.

Furthermore, the observational method offers a reflexive means of studying the studying, a way of taking Britton's (1989) sideways step into "a place in my mind ... from which I could look at things". This helps the researcher to avoid being taken in themselves, in the deceptive sense of the phrase, through the lack of another way of seeing. It offers, potentially, a reframing process to enlarge the scope of the possibilities, just as the clinical experience aims to do.

Observational methodology, then, offers a way of enhancing the objective use of subjectivity, as Hollway (1989) points out. Using this method to research psychoanalytic psychotherapy, in McGilchrist's (2009) terms, would seem to offer a way of letting the left brain, with its explicit, purposeful, categorising capacities, look at the right, with its more holistic, implicit, emotional awareness.

There are important social reasons for doing this, especially at a time of urgent need for resources that are rapidly shrinking. Once more is understood about the way in which change happens there need be less waste of human endeavour. In a child and adolescent mental health service in which I worked for some years, I could not help but notice that we as a service were under such pressure to work quickly that there was little or no time for reflection, and so we were open to being used as what Klein would call an object by the patients. That is, without the sideways step to really see what was happening and reflect on the process, we could be at risk of being caught up in acting out the dynamic in just the way the patient experienced the world, confirming their world view and entrenching the problem. Furthermore, in so far as we insist on seeing mental health problems as arising from cognition rather than wired-in relational emotion, we are ignoring the neuroscience that leads Eagleman to offer the metaphor of consciousness as a tiny stowaway on a steamship, taking credit for the journey (2011, p. 4). If consciousness is actually not at the wheel, despite what we may like to believe, it cannot be the driver of change.

On the other hand, we can work more effectively if we are prepared to accept the implications of the neuroscience about how change happens. For example, it is evident that the cost of long term psychotherapy, particularly if offered early on, can be set against a lessening of the need for huge input from youth justice and other public sector agencies. The psychotherapeutic relationship offers to take in and work through whatever trauma needs to be contained and understood, mitigating the need for it to be enacted in the public arena, and so preventing the damaging and socially expensive outcomes this entails. Furthermore, in child psychotherapy, this containment and working through is offered with the whole family in mind. Review meetings are regularly offered as a space for reflection and feedback so that engagement in the process potentially spreads throughout the family along with new ways of seeing things and thus new possibilities.

Interestingly, there are new funding initiatives that draw on this approach, which acknowledges the saving of the costs of the "road not taken" (Frost, 1916). These initiatives link with charities and local authorities in social enterprises (Cabinet Office, 2012), and look at social impact as a long term cost saving venture. I am therefore not arguing for a contemplative attitude to outcome research—far from it. It seems urgently necessary to frame the child psychotherapist's contribution to social well-being in ways that give it social and political credibility, without throwing the baby of emotional experience out with the bath-water. The way in which we use the valuable data drawn from subjective experience in clinical settings needs careful thought.

Before turning to the clinical experience, I will end this chapter with a reminder of McGilchrist's clear-sighted observation about the shaping function of attention: how what it is that exists comes into being for each one of us through interacting with our brains, so that "the idea that we could have a knowledge of it that was not also an expression of ourselves, and dependent on what we brought to the relationship is untenable" (McGilchrist, 2009, p. 37).

CHAPTER THREE

Learning the body language

Bearing in mind McGilchrist's (2009) words about the fundamental importance of the shaping role of attention, I will now turn to the clinical material from sessions that communicated the complex constellation of the feeling of being taken in. I would like to follow two strands of enquiry through the story of Dan's therapy with me, tracing both implicit process and explicit content in relation to key themes as outlined below. I hope it will be apparent that implicit process gradually became more available for explicit comment as the relationship developed. This reflexivity seems to be the particular gift of psychoanalytic psychotherapy, with its special focus on the transference of qualities from the early template onto the relationship with the therapist.

First, I offer what follows as an example of what is in everyday life the implicit process of meaning-making—how our psychobiology can objectively be seen to work towards making meaning intersubjectively, exemplified by this one case. Second, I want to explore what the feeling of being taken in might mean for a child with disturbing early experience such as Dan's. This second strand intertwines with the first, for fears and doubts about being taken in inevitably involve and affect the intersubjective process—the very mechanism of potential change, as we have seen. This had implications for Dan's progress in psychotherapy that would seem to apply for other children, too, whose early experience has been disturbing. I will consider these implications in the final chapter of the book, Changing minds.

As I explained in the introduction, the theme of being taken in seemed to encapsulate something of the central dilemma for Dan and for other fostered and adopted children—and indeed for those around them who want to help them develop: how do you take in something new when the taking-in process is compromised or damaged? The process of intersubjectivity necessitates a mutual openness, which to a child like Dan feels dangerous. Talking or acting as though it is not dangerous fails to resonate with his embodied experience; talking or acting as though it is risks triggering post-traumatic stress symptoms. Putting the absence of openness together with a wired-in and well-grounded suspicion of relationships therefore seems to preclude the possibility of growth and change. Indeed, workers with disturbed children often do report a feeling of resistance to change. As we have seen in earlier chapters of the book, emotional regulation in relationship is the very mechanism through which brain and mind grows in normal development, and through which change happens in psychotherapy. The feeling of being taken in deceptively with its deeper underlying current of feeling unable to be taken in affects this process, and so could, and sometimes does, mean that change cannot happen. What I came to think of in working with Dan as the "badly treated dog" stays outside the therapeutic relationship. This may feel safer to the child in some ways, but it also means this part cannot be looked after and helped to heal—in actual fact it perpetuates the neglect. In the clinical material that follows, this problem will be painfully evident.

There are several strands of material that powerfully represent the various qualities of Dan's implicit assumptions about being taken in. I will outline them here, before discussing the material as it happened in more detail.

Performance and imaginary worlds

There was a strong theme of performance in Dan's sessions, as I mentioned in the introduction. I will investigate the qualities of the "show" for Dan, especially in relation to his concept of ways of being together— one of which was performer and audience. His shows involved an element of theatricality, creating imaginary worlds into which I as audience was taken. One such was car world—a magical, rather glamorous but ruthless world.

Hiding, seeking, and making dens

A game of hide and seek ran through our work together in various ways—some more extreme than others. I will try to draw out the range of very different emotional qualities evoked by these. Making dens was also significant throughout the three years of our work together, dramatising aspects of what it felt like seeing and being seen, often involving infantile feelings and the explosive quality of endings.

The badly treated dog

The motif of the badly treated dog became increasingly significant, accruing symbolic complexity during the later phase of our work together. As I will try to show, it seemed to represent neglect and abuse, at times revenge, and something close to vindication. Eventually, it came to stand for the possibility of some kind of transformation.

I would like to add a caveat here: although the content carries meaning, it was a vehicle for the emotional qualities of the process, so that perhaps whichever material I chose to give in detail would have conveyed Dan's ambivalence about the prospect of being taken into relationship.

In offering this account of our work together, I've organised the material thematically and on the whole chronologically, so that particular strands can be traced as they developed, and meanings gathered around them in the context of our relationship. However, it will be apparent that there was not a sense of linear progression. In fact, these themes spiralled in and out of many sessions, and were re-visited at intervals: at different times intensely, protractedly, or fleetingly. Alongside the explicit content of the material, there was, I think, a progression as the therapy developed towards bringing the implicit qualities of the encounter into focus, which initially I found very hard to do. Perhaps it was only after quite a prolonged immersion in the new language of his world that I could really "tune in" and listen to him without losing my perspective, and thus be both receptive and reflective, making connections between feelings that were evoked, the world of his early life, and that of the therapeutic relationship.

"The lady can't see it"

From our very first week of working together there was a feeling of confusion and of "mis-steps in the dance" (Stern, 1977, p. 133). The element of performance, or the presence of a show, seemed connected to this confusion. In one of our first few sessions, having first put police cars and then pots and pans under the chair opposite me, Dan talked over my mentioning this replacement and began to wait on me. I was served in the most elaborately graceful way imaginable. It turned out that he was the hard-working chef too, getting up at one o'clock in the morning on his day off to start breakfast:

> He told me I was going to come for breakfast, lunch, and tea. Any comments about how unfair this was; about having to wait on me or about how tired the chef was and how hard he had to work to feed me got the response: "No—the lady can't see it!"

During this session, I felt Dan wanted me to believe in the performance and not see the act—suspend my disbelief as theatregoers are asked to do. It occurred to me that an audience is in the dark, and I did feel kept in the dark. There were things he did not want me to see, for example, the police cars watching me from under the opposite chair.

> Nevertheless, I talked about how he was busy feeding me—showing me how hard he feels he has to work when he is with someone; he had had to be a "waiter" for a long, long time and now he had to be the chef too, and give me breakfast, lunch, and tea. In describing what was happening, I could feel that I was addressing his nine-year-old self and not reaching a younger part of him. He evidently did not want me to speak or stop and think, and repeatedly talked over me or jumped about if he felt there was going to be a pause. It felt confusing—as if he both desperately needed and feared my full attention.

It is not putting it too strongly to say I felt compelled to concentrate on the show, on what he wanted me to see. It is hard to convey quite how vehemently, even desperately, he insisted on my not noticing what I noticed about the fact of his performance. It seemed as if he felt it would be a betrayal not to be entirely with him inside the performance. Something about his vehemence gave me a taste of the total unviability for him of the alternative; that I might not be taken into the world of the performance with him, but be outside it.

At the time, I tried to understand this in relation to a child's early need for what Bartram (2003) calls "twoness"; to be wrapped up together without intrusion from the outside world like a nursing couple before being called upon to tolerate "threeness" involving the view from outside. It may have been that what Dan, like many adopted children, had missed of the experience of a close twoness he was desperate for now, and, furthermore, dreaded its imminent withdrawal. Bartram writes that the loss of this twoness is sometimes "too great to be digested and therefore the capacity to tolerate a 'third position' is restricted or absent" (2003, p. 25). She describes struggling to judge when to let her patient have an experience of twoness, and when to intervene "to keep my own thinking alive" (ibid., p. 24). I recognise this dilemma, and also Bartram's patient's determination to keep her mind exactly where she could see it, which expressed itself in my work with Dan in an oppressive feeling of being silenced.

Dan's need of twoness was very far from being realised when it was most needed, which left him unable to manage the third position of my outside perspective, because it seemed to entail a feeling of being cast out from the closeness he desperately needed. My feeling in the room corresponded to this idea—I could feel an urgent need for my full attention on what he was showing me and on nothing that was outside that frame. I felt that noticing there was a performance would have been experienced as a betrayal.

Supervision offered another perspective on the performance material above; that of Bick's (1968) teaching that the infant feels himself to be at risk of overwhelming feelings of falling forever, or of going to pieces, without adequate parental holding. She suggests that "disturbance in the primal skin function can lead to a development of a 'second skin' formation, through which dependence on the object is replaced by a pseudo-independence" (1968, p. 56). This self-administered way of holding together, trying to self-supply what the environment lacks, is a huge and in some ways courageous effort, preferable to falling apart but born of desperation. For Dan, one function of performance seemed to be to provide a rather two-dimensional way of holding himself together in the absence of the deeper containment of which he was deprived. Like his behaviour in early contact visits, in sessions he seemed to be trying to entertain me while simultaneously communicating his suspicion that I was not fully available to him.

The waiter-chef performance thus seems to highlight the complexity of Dan's experience of the feeling of being taken in. The truth was that satisfactory twoness had not happened in Dan's early life, and so what we were experiencing in the room, close to his own early experience, actually involved an excluded and suspicious third who could not be brought in. This seems to link to the session material in which I was required not to notice the police cars that were lined up facing me under the opposite chair; Dan did not want me to think about what the police cars might stand for, watching me from under the chair, and were swiftly replaced by pots and pans. Like a magician's audience, I was not to notice the sleight of hand. I was to see only the attempts to feed and serve me, and not explicitly notice the surveillance. The implications of this were complex. One implication was that he suspected me of wrong intentions, or wrongdoing, and the prospect of my becoming aware of that seemed to feel dangerous to him. Another was that he seemed to need me to have the experience of being under surveillance in order to understand what it was like for him, for it had been part of his experience. Another may have been that in so far as he transferred his expectations of adults onto me, he was experiencing this feeling of being under surveillance in the encounter with me in the room. Yet in order to really have an experience of twoness in the sense of someone seeing things from his point of view and identifying with his feelings, paradoxically, he needed me to identify with this position of suspicious outsider, and also with being under suspicion.

I was not able to find a way to talk about this communication, as I received it during the session. It felt unsayable at the time. On the other hand, talking to him about how hard he was working as the waiter, giving me the three meals of breakfast, lunch and tea, like the three sessions of therapy, felt rather forced. My comments on what he was doing elicited his irritated remark: "No—the lady can't see it!" I mentioned that my descriptions of his hard work waiting felt as though they were aimed at the nine-year-old part of him instead of some much younger feeling that was not being attended to. Looking back, I think it prevented us focusing on the force of the switch between police surveillance and feeding, which took perhaps the better part of the next two years' work to really bring to awareness in our relationship in a regulated way.

Back in the session, after the waiter/chef came the following material:

> He got out the Play-Doh, cut some off and offered it to me, saying, "Want pizza?" There was a feeling of something insatiable, and I exclaimed how hungry this lady was. He sat on a lump of Play-Doh to flatten it—I thought of poo in a nappy. He asked if I wanted a mini pizza then rolled it up and sat on it again, squashing it down. It felt disgusting. When he asked if I wanted a piece, I said, feeling that he really would not want me to say this and that I was taking the risk of rejecting him and his offer, that maybe it would be like a poo-pizza. He looked at me with interest and smiled.

This poo-pizza could well have been his commentary on my efforts, but it also gave me an important glimpse into a feeling of something repugnant, disgusting. I think my hesitant naming of the poo-pizza did not go far enough. He behaved as if he wanted me to feel delight, but I felt disgust and could not name it; something nasty was disguised. It may have been helpful if I had had the presence of mind to verbalise the feeling of something hidden that could not be spoken about. On reflection, it seems that he was communicating a sense of himself as a baby who was too disgusting to be taken in. Tellingly, this too was a feeling that I could not put into words; there was much that was unspeakable at that early point in the work.

However, there may have been value for Dan in my experiencing the real discomfort of unsayability without the release of being able to put it into words straight away. I might then have felt to him, and to myself, that I was somewhat outside the experience—had wrapped my mind around it, as it were, too soon.

Our difficulty, then, was that in order to help him take in and come to terms with the truth of his experience, I had to be aware of, to take in, what he felt he needed to exclude from awareness as too dangerous. There was a technical difficulty in finding a way to indicate my awareness that felt tolerable to him. Meltzer (1976) has written about notions of temperature and distance in relation to this question, and Alvarez (2004) has considered ways of "finding the wavelength". The problem of "making the thought thinkable" (Alvarez, 1993) was vividly present in working with Dan. It seemed that most of all he needed to really feel the qualities of his early experience that constituted his template for relating as it emerged in his experience in the room with me.

As the months went by there was still confusion, but the qualities of the space into which he felt he was being taken in sessions became clearer, as he began to let the lady see it. The frightening question of who this lady was that was doing the seeing became apparent. The following session came after three months' work.

"Who are you?"

On coming into the room, he immediately got the football out of his box and began to kick it around the room aggressively. He seemed furious, and I said that something was certainly getting kicked around. He quickly got more and more manic, sending the football hurtling against the window blinds. It felt very hostile.

There followed a conversation to do with having to miss athletics after school and looking forward to going bowling that I found confusing. As I tried to understand what he meant, and connect it to what was happening here, he was still kicking the ball around hard—hitting the ceiling, walls, and blind. I had the strong feeling that asking about it was not helping him, but neither had sitting quietly watching. I was evidently not "getting it".

Then he got the marbles and started to throw them, smiling a forced and rather chilling smile as he did so. I intervened here, and he substituted Play-Doh. He seemed excited rather than angry now, getting carried away; I think he would have found it hard to stop. He threw the lump of Play-Doh at the light, and I took it and said I thought he needed me to help him stop now as it was getting a bit wild. I wondered if he would grab the Play-Doh from my hands, but he seemed to settle for a moment. He was still holding a little bit of Play-Doh, and he flattened it over the lock of the cupboard. I wondered what a covered lock might mean for him: can't get in? Can't get out? People can't see in?

His initial fury may well have been to do with holding me responsible for his having to come to therapy and missing athletics after school, even though this was confused by the fact that we met in the mornings. I was not able to form this idea in my mind at the time, but in retrospect I think his rightful need to have someone take responsibility for all that he had missed and continued to miss out on was infuriatingly complicated by his sense of fairness—he could not even directly accuse me in the way that he needed to.

He got a blanket and put it over his head. He walked towards me in monster mode saying strange words then asked in a monster voice, "Who are you?" I tried to voice his fears about who I might be—this strange lady who said strange things. I then worried that putting it into words made it more frightening for him. Perhaps it did, for he then tried to put the blanket over my head, which I prevented. He opened the cupboard and climbed inside. I said he wanted to hide himself away—maybe it was very scary thinking about the monster. As he curled up on the top shelf space with its hard edges, it felt horrible.

My not getting it about how angry he was with me for what he had missed and was missing seems to have escalated the force of feeling. There seemed to be a frightening sense of a monster in the room and a need to be shut away. He seems to have been communicating something about an internalised world, present in the room in the transference, in which hostility necessitates being shut away. The emotional flavour of the being shut away was complex, involving a feeling of horrible punishment, but there was also something of a protective impulse, though whether this was directed towards himself or towards me was hard to distinguish.

Looking back, I think an important step was missing here; he had expressed hostility, but I had not received the communication and really taken it in in relation to me as his object. There was a monster in the room, but where was it located? He punished himself, shut away in the harsh restricted space of the top shelf of the cupboard, but perhaps the person he really wanted to punish, or rather, needed to hold responsible was me in the transference, as representing the qualities of his early experience, embodied now in relation to the adults in his life. My omission left him with the hatred, and furthermore, with a reinforced feeling that the relationship with his object could not survive the direct force of his hostility.

My hesitant naming of the question of the "strange lady", and worries about who I might be, does seem to have scared him. He responded by wanting to put the blanket over my head, before climbing into the cupboard when I prevented that. No wonder the space in the cupboard was extremely uncomfortable. It seems that he could not feel fully taken into a safe place until he had experienced me taking in, without retaliation, the force of his hatred as directed towards me. There is an element of this in the session, implicitly, in that I was still available to him after his having thrown marbles at me, but I did not explicitly accept the force of his hatred towards me until some time later in the therapy, as I will try to show, when I think he found it helpful.

It may be illuminating to give the material that followed getting out of the cupboard.

> There was a sequence of play about a car that was trying to escape because it had stolen something. It was pursued by a police car, and went to hide in a little wooden play house. That wasn't enough protection, so Dan piled on two big cushions and two blankets. However, even this wasn't enough: the police car had the helicopter on its side and the helicopter turned out to have a saw that cut through the cushions and blankets to get to the hiding place. It felt vicious. I said there seemed to be absolutely nowhere safe for this little car to hide, and, feeling nervous and unsure whether naming this would be helpful or not, I tried to link it to what had happened in our session, and how frightened he may have been about what I "saw". I suggested that he may feel that what I saw was a very bad boy who threw things, and not a boy who felt scared sometimes. Then he said he needed the loo, and I felt I'd overdone it.

The difficulty of processing these fearful feelings with such a quality of imminent danger is apparent. In keeping my comments in the play, I could seem to be abrogating responsibility; in naming my role in his fears, I could exacerbate his terror and trigger a primitive response, bypassing his prefrontal cortex, cutting out thought before action, and directly activating the fright response of his amygdala. What I tried to do in the session material above was to walk a narrow tightrope, which hinted at a link with the session, but identified the fear and not the monstrous badness that was felt to cause it—which I experienced in the room as the viciousness of the saw. He immediately needed to leave the room at that point to go to the loo. Even beginning to approach the nature of it felt inflammatory, and the room seemed to become intolerable for him so that he felt the urgent need to leave. When you have been that frightened, you cannot bear to be reminded of it—and yet it inescapably infuses your body until it can be mediated by someone else.

During this first phase of therapy, it was therefore very hard for Dan to stay in the room with me. He repeatedly left the room to go to the loo or get water, or escape down the corridor. Sometimes this extended a game of hide and seek that I will discuss shortly, but sometimes it felt more extreme; for example, he would make a dash for the fire exit or switch all the lights off in the corridor, or push the emergency call button. There was evidently a feeling of danger for Dan in connection with being taken into the therapy room with me. If we were to begin to make connections between the world of his past and that of his present, we needed to explore the qualities of who I was for him with great caution on my part and courage on his.

The car that was trying to escape was an important communication, coming as it did immediately after the stint in the cupboard. The fact that Dan portrayed the car as having stolen something seems noteworthy, as if he was in touch with a feeling of having been deprived of something. Increasingly over time, there was a sense of entitlement in session material associated with stealing, in line with Winnicott's (1946) ideas about deprivation and delinquency as a sign of hope, rightfully addressing a need. At this early stage, however, getting what you need was a covert business associated with the terrifying prospect of being hunted down for punishment.

This seems to link with the need for a cover-up show; for example, the winning performance of the waiter in the early session quoted above, to distract attention from what he seems to have experienced as a crime—a kind of robbery. Thus, being taken into therapy and receiving my attention was a complex, ambivalent, frightening experience for him, associated with lots of fears about what I might see and about the qualities of the person doing the seeing. The symbol he used of a persecuting and relentless cutting saw portrays this graphically. Again, as in the poo-pizza material, there is confusion about who might be felt to be the source of the problem. The saw may have represented potentially not just his object, but a part of him that would be enraged to fully see and keep in view what had been taken—perhaps felt to have been robbed—from him. It may be that not seeing/not being seen was his way of trying to maintain a fragile equilibrium. Being taken into therapy necessitated being seen, and thus posed a threat to this fragile equilibrium that was felt to be very dangerous.

Material from a session a month later seems to clarify the feeling of danger associated in Dan's mind and body with being taken in, precipitating his urgent need to get out of the room.

"Safe in here"

In a session after one missed through my illness, he began by tipping over an armchair, examining it, then crawling underneath it.

It wasn't quite big enough. I felt that he wanted somewhere to be tucked safely away, and felt sad for him that he was getting too big. I said something along these lines—about wanting somewhere to be safely tucked in but maybe worried that he might be too big now.

He spotted the table as an alternative and crawled underneath it, curling up. I said it looked as if he might like to be a baby safely curled up in a mum's tum so that we would never have to be apart. He said, "You forgot me". I said that when I was away last session he felt as though I had dropped him and forgotten all about him. I said I thought it was very hard for him to think that he might be safely tucked up in my mind, even though we were not in the same room; hard to think I might be wondering about whether he was OK and what he was up to, keeping him in my mind when we were not in the room together.

The curled up place then became a den, and he began to use strange language. I said perhaps he needed me to know what it feels like to be on the outside, not sure what might be going on—maybe my words sound like a foreign language sometimes.

Looking back, this response to my remarks about keeping him in mind suggests that he felt them to be inflammatory. The space to curl up in turned into a den. Something potentially protective became defensive, even hostile, emanating strange words. This may have happened because part of him apprehended and responded to the idea of a mind to hold him, but it was too painful to contemplate given both the tremendous loss in the past, and the prospect of the almost immediate loss of it now in the ending of the session.

However, it also seems likely that my words made no sense to another part of him. This part may have actively wanted to reject such a possibility as meaningless, for contemplating such a close connection as desirable would bring his inner world into turmoil, if it was organised on the principle that guarded separation is necessary for survival. My countertransference feeling was of exclusion, which may connect with ideas about twoness and threeness discussed in relation to the "lady can't see it" session, and may well have had a link with the missed session. It may be that as soon as he began to apprehend the possibility of being held in mind, the interruptions were unbearable.

He asked me to cover him up and I put a blanket over the tabletop. "Put something here, where my hand is", he told me. I pulled the blanket across and said he wanted not to have anyone see him. Then he asked for his box, and wanted me to make it darker because it was still too light. I said I could not make it dark enough for him— the light would still get in. He said, "It's safe in here". It felt genuine for that moment, and I said "You feel safe in there." He said, "Night night", and made loud snoring noises. I said it sounded like someone sleeping, but they seemed to be doing it very loudly to make sure someone thinks they're asleep. I could hear him rustling about while he made the snoring noises, and wondered aloud what he might be doing while he was pretending to be asleep. Then he threw out a lump of Play-Doh, and then another, and made baby noises. I said it sounded like there was a baby in there who was throwing lumps of stuff out. He threw another lump and said it was yucky stuff. I said there was yucky stuff around, and the baby was throwing it at me.

He said, "Now I can play with my dinosaurs", and I wondered about the link between throwing out what felt like lumps of shit and beasts from ancient history. A phrase from a boy I worked with years ago came to mind about "people from the old days" who came and wreaked havoc. Dan said in a deep, gruff, angry voice that the bad baby was going to get whacked because he had lost his nappy. I said the baby had lost his nappy, and now the man was angry with him and was going to hurt him. He told me the baby had dropped the nappy on purpose, and I said that although the baby was so little it seemed like things were still the baby's fault. He said the man was looking for a whip to whack the bad baby's bottom with. I had a picture very vividly brought to mind of a little child with a bare bottom about to be hit. I said it was very cruel that the man was going to whack the baby's bottom with a whip, and then felt unsure whether Dan could hear this at the moment or whether he was identifying more with the man.

This then was the place into which Dan took me in sessions, and into which he felt himself to be taken, linked to a feeling of having been forgotten. My missing a session evoked the neglect and cruelty of his early childhood in which he seemed to experience the neglect and cruelty as being his own fault for being bad. He seemed to re-experience in this session the dangers of cruel punishment for the "bad baby", but in a way that suggested the possibility of an identification with the cruel man figure.

I would now like to explore the link between neglect (as experienced in the therapy by missed sessions) and Dan's capacity to take in the possibility of a shared world with different qualities. In order to investigate this connection, I offer some material from a session a few weeks later that took place after two sessions missed because of illness in Dan's family.

"Our town", Spiderman, and the Incredible Hulk

In the introduction, I mentioned the imaginary worlds that Dan created and into which I was taken in sessions. It seemed to be crucial to the therapy for me to be taken into the world of Dan's mind if he was eventually to feel himself to be fully taken into mine. As we have seen, the alternative seemed to be a kind of performance in which we were together as audience and performer, and he had the job of entertaining me. The following session shed light on this dynamic. It took place five months into the therapy after the two missed sessions I have mentioned.

> He began by smiling in a rather brittle way, and saying, "You weren't there". I agreed seriously that I wasn't there when it was time for us to meet up. He seemed satisfied with this and then went to the desk and sat down, telling me to "budge up closer". He spotted my glasses and tried them on, passing me his to hold. He said he hated his, and I registered the strength of this feeling. I then said maybe he wondered what it's like looking through my eyes.

I felt he was showing me not just that he hated his glasses, but that he hated what people saw when they looked at him. This may well have had a link in his mind with the two missed sessions; it may have been his unconscious explanation for why I had not been able to "see" him. The glasses seemed to stand for a view of him that was hated and hateful; a view I needed to take in if I was to take in his internal world so he could feel taken in in an authentic way. He seemed by this stage to want to "budge up closer" as he invited me to do at the beginning. The evidence of what follows suggests that trying on my glasses may have symbolised the growing appeal to him of the possibility of a new way of looking that was shared rather than oppositional.

> He nodded briefly but changed the subject, saying, "What shall we make for our town?" I registered that we were making somewhere together, a town that would belong to both of us, and said,

"We-ell … let's think …" He told me, "I like it when you do that".
I asked what he liked, and he said it was when I said "We-ell …",
and he copied my tone of voice. He told me it was like CBeebies,
although he liked CBBC. I said that although he was nine now and
liked older things like CBBC, a younger bit of him still liked it when
I said things in a CBeebies-type way. He said yes.

He wasn't sure what to make, and then suddenly grabbed a bit
of paper, folded it in half, and started cutting out a double rectangle, saying, "I know!" I was curious to know what it might be. As
he cut, he talked to me in the made-up language he sometimes used
and seemed to want me to try it out. I repeated the word to him and
he corrected me, amused. We batted the sounds to and fro between
us till he was happy with the way I said it, and I said something
about trying to learn his language. He smiled at me and it felt good,
like a moment in which something was understood between us,
and he said, "You are, you're learning, girl!"

There were moments during the therapy when "his language" felt
purposefully excluding, as if the point was to convey how meaningless
my words felt to him sometimes—as if I was in my own little world
without him when I talked, and he wanted me to know what that felt
like. However, this felt different. It felt as if there was a hope that we
could get back together again after a gap, and I would take responsibility for us not being able to get together, and try to tune in again to his
language. This seemed to usher in the idea of a shared world, represented by "our town" in which his younger "CBeebies" feelings could
be taken into account.

However, his ambivalence about what kind of world this was soon
emerged.

He started to write a "p" on the paper rectangle he'd cut out, and
then changed his mind and turned it over, writing "karate". He
passed it to me to read, and I did, remarking how quickly he had
changed his mind—I wondered what he was going to put before,
beginning with "p". He said, "Pizza". I said something like, "Hmm,
that's interesting, pizza turns into karate very quickly—before the
word is even written. So a place where you get fed turns into a
place where there's kicking and self defence". He said yes.

He then said what the town needed was an airport. I wondered
aloud about what that need for an airport might be about. He

folded a piece of paper in half and put it on the page like a tent. He
told me to write on it that a plane was leaving in ten minutes. I said
it looked like it might be a departures board that tells people when
planes are leaving, and he agreed. I said maybe he was showing us
both that it seemed like just when he got settled somewhere it felt
like he was going to have to go away soon. He asked me to add
some more to the list of planes leaving any minute, and I said perhaps he was showing me that people are setting off very soon, with
hardly any time left to be together; there seems to be no time to get
settled—everyone has to rush off very quickly to catch their plane.
I said that perhaps it was a bit like our sessions—all that coming
and going. Perhaps as soon as he gets settled and we start getting
on with something together it feels like time to go. He said yes.

He said we needed to make a plane now, and I said there seemed
to be something about wanting a plane—did the people want to get
away sometimes? He said they did, and handed the sheet of paper
to me, indicating that I should draw the plane, saying he was rubbish at it. I said he was telling me he felt he was rubbish at it, but I
wondered if he thought I would think what he drew was rubbish.
He smiled and drew a spindly little plane, a bit like a rocket. He
handed it to me to cut out. He smiled and rather bashfully said he
wanted to throw it away. I said he felt like throwing it away, but
perhaps he was hoping that I wouldn't want to throw it away but
would want to keep it. I was holding it as I spoke and he seemed
touched.

He got the sellotape and began to wind it around my chair and
the desk. I said, "I get it, I'm not going anywhere", and he repeated,
"You're not going anywhere!" delightedly. As he worked, I said
perhaps he hated the fact that sessions had to end, and I thought
he wanted to keep me here; maybe this was the only way he could
think of to keep me here—by sticking me with sellotape. I told him
I thought it might be really hard for him to think for a minute that I
would want to be here with him if he didn't stick me down.

He wound it more and more extravagantly around my chair
and the desk, and then began to wind it around my wrists, which I
allowed, and my ankles, which I didn't. I acknowledged how much
he wanted to make sure I couldn't go anywhere, and said I would
have to stay right here. He smiled and said yes. He carried on sticking the sellotape to everything he could think of: the doll's house,

the door, the cupboard. It was sad watching him, and the sellotape didn't stick on the door well enough to hold the tension of the next stretch. I said the sellotape wasn't strong enough, and perhaps he wished he had a stronger way than sellotape to hold onto people and stop them going.

He smiled cunningly and said it was a trap he was making, and I said maybe he felt that making me stay meant he had to trap me, because it was so hard to believe I might want to stay otherwise. He said he was Spiderman and repeated that he was making a trap, and I realised I hadn't got it the first time. He laughed in a mischievous way.

Looking back, I think my remark about his having to trap me was misattuned, and so he told me he was Spiderman, a figure with superpowers, to give me another chance to try and get the message. It was not so much that he had to trap me but that he wanted to to shift the power balance a bit. It seemed important for Dan to move away quite quickly from the feelings of sadness that were around, when the sellotape was not strong enough. Then, after Spiderman, came the Incredible Hulk.

He started chopping through the sellotape and said the Incredible Hulk was here now. It was towards the end of the session, and as he waded about looking big and karate chopping through the sellotape, I wondered aloud if maybe the incredible hulk made it easier to take things apart when they'd been together? He karate chopped through as much of the sellotape as he could, with an air of rescue, and I unwound my wrists. I said that it looked as though the Incredible Hulk was trying to rescue me from Spiderman's web.

I told him I thought it might be really important to look at our calendar together in a minute and see when we were meeting next, because I wondered if the Incredible Hulk might think that once links were chopped through they could never come back together again. We looked at the calendar and saw that we were meeting the next day. He told me the Incredible Hulk would be back tomorrow.

The link between the pizza, so quickly replaced by karate, and then a plane departure, the sellotape, Spiderman and the Incredible Hulk was fascinating. He seemed to be representing symbolically the fears and dangers of being taken into a shared world in which he had a hope of being nourished. There seemed to be a worry that his aggression, connected perhaps to having to wait too long, meant people would leave, and thus had to be stuck into place. There also seemed to be something about his own wanting to be able to leave. His sense of his own capacity to keep people was that it was insufficient; they seemed to have to be stuck down. This would fit with an early template for relating set by neglect and being passed around the birth family, before being placed in a foster home and then an adoptive family. The sadness of this predicament seemed to be too much to stay with, and so he resorted to an identification with Spiderman, a figure with superpowers. Spiderman's web, though, precipitated the appearance of the Incredible Hulk; a figure who transforms through anger into somebody huge, green, and monstrous. Yet his role in the play seemed intended to be helpful, releasing me from Spiderman's binding web. Was he, I wonder, felt to be containing all the anger, swelling to huge proportions, so as not to inflict it on the internal mother figure felt to be trapped and helpless?

> It was time to finish, and we walked back to mum in the waiting room. Mum said sorry about the missed sessions earlier in the week, she'd been ill. Dan looked at me and smiled in an anxious placatory way as if I'd been wrongly blamed, and said, "So that was the reason!" I looked at him and nodded, feeling that it was OK, and he looked relieved.

Our exchange of looks conveyed a mutual sense of "you know that I know". This unspoken sharing of awareness was perhaps an example of Braten's (2008) intersubjective attunement. I think my look may have conveyed to him that it was all right; I would not retaliate for the reproach that he had transferred onto me about not getting together for the missed sessions. It seems that children like Dan, whose expectations of relationships are adapted to adversity, need someone to take compassionate responsibility for the failures of their objects in order to internalise a more robust object and begin to relate differently. However, both content and process are important here; this unspoken exchange shows that by this stage we had established the beginnings of an implicit non-verbal attunement—seeing through each other's eyes as he had done symbolically in trying on my glasses at the start of this session.

"You say wow!"

Following on from its appearance at the beginning of our work together, the graceful waiter performance recurred frequently, with its undercurrent of sewage. It seemed to be his way of letting me know how hard it was to disentangle the confusion about whose need was being satisfied in sessions. Furthermore, the hopeful desire to be a lovely baby, capable of evoking delight, seemed to cause him some pain, and competed with the feeling that he was the "bad baby"—not at all the kind of baby who can be taken in and looked after, and so it was better not to hope, but to protect himself from the anguish of disappointment by doing it all himself. The complexity of this was exemplified in a session after about six months' work:

> He spotted some new Play-Doh along with the old, and gave me a rather sing-song "Thank you!" This felt like a mixture of the genuine and the formulaic, as if the childlike "say thank you" formulation did briefly express something for him. He examined the old Play-Doh, and told me it still had bits in it that needed to come out, while starting to play with it. I said although there were bits and it was not perfect, it looked like it could still be used. A little while later, as he played, he said to himself: "It doesn't have to be thrown away just because it's yucky".

Maybe the sing-song "thank you" for the new Play-Doh, which seemed part heartfelt and part forced or formulaic, represented a complicated mixture of positive and negative feelings that were impossible to sort out, like the old and new Play-Doh he combined. I said that the Play-Doh was still useable because he had started to use it, but I now feel this remark pre-empted a development that had not yet happened—a sense of something compromised but workable that perhaps had still not yet been fully established two years later. Perhaps more to the point would have been an exploration of the feeling of something "yucky" that had to be hidden, disguised or misrepresented, along with the concomitant feeling of being deceived. This material seems to link with the poo-pizza material that reminded me of a baby's filled nappy. He had already shown me how he felt himself to be the "yucky" baby who was thrown away.

Sorting out good and bad, old and new, things that were to be kept, and things that were to be thrown away was the work of the following two and a half years of therapy. In his final session, he did sort through his box and folders and decide what he wanted to keep, what to throw away, what I was to keep, and what "the children" could have. In this first stage of the therapy, things were much more entangled and confused, but after six months it was evident at times that he was engaged in the process of trying to sort out the confusion. Later in the session I have quoted from above:

> He said he was being a chef, and told me I could not see him in the game, but could in real life—the first time he had made that distinction. He made a cake for me, very carefully and beautifully, out of old and new Play-Doh; the old was the filling and decoration.

He had earlier used the word "yucky" about the old Play-Doh filling and decoration for the cake, and although the associations were faecal, like the poo-pizza, the word was used in the context of something to eat.

The correlation between psychic and physical taking in has been studied from the earliest days of psychoanalysis. There is not space here to do justice to this huge area, touching on symbol formation and on serious physical symptoms like eating disorders. However, Abraham's patient who when he was a little boy "had the idea that loving somebody was exactly the same as the idea of eating something good" (1916, p. 257) reminds me of Dan, who had the opposite experience. Dan told me later about having been given bad milk as a baby; his experience of loving connection to others was laced with danger. He may well have felt in the cake material quoted above that he was being asked to swallow something dangerous and disgusting in the session and pretend it was good. It might have been helpful if I had been able to talk to him about this, rather than just feel it, but still after six months' work it was as if for Dan and for me too a kind of embargo applied, and it was not yet talkable. Maybe this relates to the feeling of confusion that was around, which may have been a mask for a question about who might be the source of something disgusting.

Schimmenti's (2012) writing about shame is relevant here. He sees an understanding of shame as "critical for evaluating the psychic functioning of patients who have experienced parental neglect or abuse", and illustrates "how emotional neglect and intense role reversal can lead to negative expectations of interpersonal relationships, disturbing feelings of shame, and a sense of a defective self" (Schimmenti, 2012, p. 195).

It would thus have been helpful to claim the shittiness more in relation to me and the weekly therapy-cake with its sessions and gaps, rather than leaving Dan with the fear and shame of suspecting himself to be the unlovably shitty baby. It made for a complicated constellation. I think he felt he needed a smokescreen for his fierce desire for revenge: a stance of "I am doing something lovely for you (but really it's disgusting)", which might perhaps compound his sense of unlovableness—even if it stoked a feeling of secret triumph of having "got one over" on me. The nature of what is taken in is suspect and heavily disguised. This seems to be the way it is experienced by Dan, whether he is on the giving or receiving end of this transaction—he was showing me a world in which something bad was presented as good, which necessitated disguise and deception. In fact, as I have mentioned, he later talked about the "bad milk" that he was fed as a child. Thus, at a primitive oral level, with its psychic parallel, Dan's experience had taught him it was not safe to swallow what he was given.

This was conveyed in the above session when he made the cake, carefully and elaborately, out of old and new Play-Doh. It had a complicated feeling about it, as if something was being masked—reminiscent of the poo-pizza session in the first week. I felt he was showing me he wanted to make something nice for me but somehow slip in the "old stuff" Play-Doh, which had a distinctly faecal feel. Our last session had been difficult and chaotic, and it did seem that he was making some kind of reparative effort, although complicated and compromised by the insertion of the "old stuff".

In the reversal of the feeding role, and its partial corruption with faecal material, I think Dan was showing me complex interacting layers of disturbing feelings of shame, fear of abandonment for being defective, protection against this by taking the feeding role, and, furthermore, a fierce but furtive desire for revenge in relation to this question. That there was something furtive was evident when he insisted the cake had to be cooked outside the room in the corridor:

> I wondered aloud about this cooking place; why did it need to be outside? He did not answer this directly, but hurried towards the door. I said that it looked like he felt something needed to be removed from the room, but I thought we needed to try and stay in the room together and see if we could manage to do the cake stuff in here. He accepted this, putting the cake near the door instead

and telling me that would be the cooking place. He danced across the room, carrying the plate with flair and a bit of a flourish, and I was struck by his graceful physicality. I said he was dancing, and noticed that he carried the plates behind his back. He told me: "You say Wow!" I did say wow because I felt delighted by him, alongside something more complicated that was perhaps to do with disguised oppression. I said he was showing me something pretty clever, and I was to be quite impressed with what he could do—all that work he was forced to do, cooking and waiting—so hard but he was making it look easy, turning it into a dance. I was genuinely impressed by his graceful performance.

His "You say Wow!" was poignant. I did say "Wow!", and felt, among other things, there was something essential in him to be celebrated in that moment. It may be that I was taken in, in the deceptive sense, by a performance he may not have felt was authentic. However, he may have needed me to be "taken in" at some level, while also at another level needing me not to be; to be aware that the performance was not the whole story. I did realise there was a strong element of "yucky stuff" secreted into the performance, carried behind his back, but just as a new parent often does not mind their baby's dirty nappy as much as another person might, I felt well-disposed towards him, even as he was preparing the cake with its subtext. There is a question about whether it would have been helpful to be able to name what was hidden behind his back and also in the cake more than I did. Stern (2004) writes about the shift from the experience of the present moment to putting it into words the moment after. He suggests that this more distant position only appears to objectify the experience, when "actually it is still a first-person experience about trying to take a third-person stance relative to something that just happened" (2010, p. 33). On this occasion, the shared experience did seem to facilitate something being taken in, for Dan was then able to show some vulnerability more openly:

> Shortly after this exchange, the cakes became difficult to carry and he struggled for a few moments. I felt an impulse to offer help. Then he said, "I need help!" and I came and helped him, noticing aloud that he had a lot to carry and it was hard to balance. He said he had rescued them and I agreed. I said he had a lot on his plate and he accepted this.

In this interchange, he seemed to be on the verge of taking me into his private world in which he was needy, and to allow himself to be taken into a relationship in which he could be cared for and helped. He did, however, need then to represent what happened to both of us as his having rescued something, and I think this was valid. I did not pre-empt his call for help by offering first, although the impulse was there. He was thus the author of the rescue. He was perhaps facilitated in this by feeling held in a relationship that could apprehend positive and negative aspects of his personality; could take in the performance and the poo, even though at this stage the second was done mostly implic-itly for fear of reinforcing his shame.

In working with Dan, I have mentioned the imaginary theatrical worlds into which I was taken. One of these was "car world". This next excerpt from a session that took place about a year into the therapy, shortly after his tenth birthday, exemplifies some of the qualities of this world.

Stuntman and car world

Dan began the session by talking about my town where he came for sessions: "a strange place" not like his town. As he spoke, he stretched out between the chair and table, forming a kind of bridge with his body that did not quite reach. I said maybe it felt like there were two different worlds, and he was stretched between them. It looked like maybe he felt in danger of falling, I said with some feeling, gesturing at his precarious stretch. He did not want me to say this and scrambled off the chair in an irritated way, shaking his head. He nearly did fall and I helped him get down, saying that although he did have someone here to help with the stretch—me, it did not seem to be much use. He hurried over to the cupboard, saying, "Teatime!"

We were back with the waiter, who was as attentive as ever, and, fur-thermore, this time only had the use of one arm. Dan seemed to be using the waiter to try and protect himself against the danger of being another kind of waiter, waiting between sessions. At these times, I think he felt himself to be in an extremely precarious situation between two worlds, physically demonstrated in this session by the stretch of his body between chair and table as he talked about my town and his. The issue of bringing together two worlds, old and new, is hugely problematic for adopted children, especially those who have been adopted after significant time in birth and foster families, as Dan had been. Fagan (2011) writes about the conflicting sets of relationships for late adopted children, and the difficulties in bringing two worlds together. She suggests that they can struggle to know what is real and alerts us to the "desperate jumble and collapse of the past and the present, as damaged and inadequate internal objects from the past vie with new introjections" (Fagan, 2011, p. 131). Good and bad, old and new, are hopelessly intermingled like the Play-Doh with bits in it that cannot be removed.

In the world of the waiter that he turned to after the risk of falling, once again, there was a cowpat-cake. This time, I was a bit more able to talk with him about the feeling that I might be forced to eat it and pretend it was a lovely cake.

> I also wondered with him about a link between the cake and the stretch between the two towns and the danger of falling between them, suggesting that it seemed that as soon as he began to feel something good might be on offer, there was a fear of falling into the gap in its absence when he felt no one was there to catch him. I tried to put into words the possibility that his way of trying to remedy this was to try to bridge the gap himself, and turn the waiting child into the kind of waiter who served food, which was bound to be tainted. It occurred to me that the cake might be heavily overlaid with feelings about his birthday the previous weekend. I said that he had just had a birthday, and here we were with a cake—what might the cake be showing us about what his birthday felt like?

I think these wonderings of mine—even if they did describe his experience, or possibly because they did get near it, were too much for him—an overdose. It may be that I was so keen to show I had taken in what he was showing me that I was not identifying sufficiently with the pain of it. In response to what I had said, he became rather manic.

> He parked a motorbike in the cake and tried hard to fix a stuntman on to it. My heart sank; it felt mindless. I thought of a world of motorbikes and stuntmen he had shown me before that we had come to call car world, where danger is faced carelessly and no one registers hurt. I said it looked hard to get him on the bike, and suggested that maybe things were not working too well for the stuntman just now.

He set him precariously on top of a line of felt pens representing candles. I said it looked like he was a kind of offering up there on the cake candles—even a sacrifice. He might burn but he just had to lie there; I wondered why. He put more felt pens in a circle, saying that he would be safer. I did not feel he was safe. I felt he was showing me a world in which stoic suffering is glorified. An image of a motor-cyclist on a stunt called the wall of death came to mind. It struck me that maybe it was not about safety at all, it was about daring and self-sacrifice and what danger he could bear alone. As he brought the cake over to show me, I said something like, "I think maybe you're bringing me the stuntman and hoping I'll think he's pretty great, high up there on the candles". He brought the cake over to present before me with a flourish. I said that was quite a performance—he was not noticing the danger; I was not to notice the danger. I was to be impressed, but meanwhile stuntman would get burned.

Looking back on this session is painful. It was the first one after a birth-day, and it seems now that I had perhaps confirmed his worst fears about being neglected by not giving him a present, or indeed being present. Again, looking back, it would have been helpful to find a way to acknowledge the pain I had inflicted by seeming not to care about him in not giving him a present/presence on his birthday. Unfortunately, I was not able to come anywhere near voicing or even feeling this in the session. In fact, at the time, I had the feeling that I was not impor-tant enough to him for it to matter whether or not I had given him a present. The idea that I might matter to him, either as myself or as a representation of key adults in his life, would have felt to me like an aggrandisement. In retrospect, I think this feeling was an important communication about our relationship, letting me know that experience had taught Dan that letting people matter was a dangerous enterprise to be avoided at all costs. The world of the stuntman seemed to offer him a kind of psychic retreat (Steiner, 1993) that protected him from feeling the extreme suffering of starvation and neglect, represented by the burning candles, though it prevented him developing a more genuinely resilient relationship with reality. Stuntman seemed to kick into gear and manically triumph, surviving torture, soon after a neglected birthday and a feeling of falling with no one to help.

Perhaps retreating to a stuntman performance of extreme and unacknowledged danger was Dan's way of coping with an internal world in which there was no order—anything could happen. Dan's sense of himself as a daredevil survivor against the odds seemed to be an organising principle, without which he feared imminent and utter collapse. My promptings about safety and protection seemed wide of the mark. I think he wanted me to see him as strong, and to recognise the strength and toughness that he did in fact have, and felt he had to have, as well as the fantasy toughness that protected him from psychic pain but prevented his development and relating in fuller ways.

For Dan, I think there was a desperate struggle to prevent his hatred and resentment about this state of affairs breaking out and destroying everything. Perhaps he felt it could only be leaked out in heavy disguise—the cowpat cake—in order to preserve the hope of something more loving, against overwhelming odds. He did not seem to have much faith that I would withstand the full force of his fury. In the transference, I think I was experienced as rather fragile and easily broken. The stuntman who was prepared to face danger and death and gloried in the sacrifice may have been his way of coping with this situation and protecting his objects—me as the neglectful mother in the transference, forgetting his birthday—from the vengeance he may have wished to inflict. In car world no one was ever really damaged and no one could be hurt, although there were terrible crashes and collisions in mid-air. People fell in slow motion, and gang members would come to their rescue. I think this seemed to him a more reliable protection than my intermittent efforts. Like the one—armed waiter, he would rather manage without. However, interestingly, noticing that the stuntman's performance might mean he got burnt was followed by a performance of his own:

> He told me he was going to do a performance, and began to do a dance routine—pretty agile and a bit flash—singing a Michael Jackson song and changing the words to say "blame it on the boobies", which struck me as pretty direct. I felt like a tantalising booby mother, who seemed to offer good things that were really bad. I remembered the "bad milk" that he had told me he was fed as a child. He seemed excited and rather manic. I suggested that he was telling me the boobies have a lot to answer for. He smiled and carried on singing, but when the session had to end he grabbed wildly at whatever he could, throwing things about and tipping things out. I talked about how he felt like I was cruelly chucking him out and getting rid of him, even after his performance. This seemed to

calm him down a bit, and he nodded. Instead of trashing the rest of the room as he had often done in the past, he was able to stop and check when we were next meeting.

This performance pointed at a source of the trouble other than himself: "blame it on the boobies". Dan had previously talked about Michael Jackson as someone who had suffered in early life and then done what he called stupid things. In identification with him, Dan could blame it on the boobies, which felt like quite a direct accusation, and a reasonable thing to do in the circumstances. His performance was excited, but had lost the quality of torture and sacrifice that characterised the stuntman on the candles. I am not sure what effected this change; it may have been that he felt I did occasionally "get it"; it may have been that my talking about a performance that ignored the stuntman's suffering meant he was less caught up inside it. No wonder he felt angry that the session had to end so soon after this song—perhaps he felt I was getting rid of him for daring to blame it on the boobies, even though it was dressed up in an engaging performance. In his reaction to the ending he seemed to be conveying his anger about how impossible he felt it was to be really taken in emotionally in a lasting way, despite his best efforts to impress and delight. He did seem calmed, though, by my acknowledgement of this. Klein's (1940) work on the relationship between mourning and manic depressive states of mind suggests that beginning to acknowledge the failures of the object, in a relationship he felt could withstand this, may have lessened the intensity of his manic defence.

To put it another way, towards the end of the first year of therapy, the new world of our relationship was beginning to become possible through my mostly implicit acceptance of the world he was showing me in sessions; the world of his early childhood, which he conveyed in powerful states of mind/feeling. Occasionally, when he was able to feel that I could take these feelings without retaliation or collapse, like when I said that it felt like I was cruelly chucking him out after his "blame it on the boobies" performance, he could live in the present; he stopped trashing the room, noticed where we were, and checked when we were next meeting.

However, despite these advances, Dan tested my limits and the limits of the room ferociously and often. He would frequently run out of the room or press the alarm bell. This may have been a sign that there was huge conflict about where the monstrous badness I have mentioned earlier was felt to reside; often, badness was not felt to be outside, but inside the room. We have seen that his response seemed to be the human sacrifice position of stuntman, which necessitated tremendous physical courage in an internal world in which a powerful destructive force seemed to be prevalent in the absence of supportive good figures. Though as the previous session showed, by this stage there did seem to be the beginnings of a consolidation of a shift from the stuntman state of mind with its disguised attacks towards a feeling that the relationship may be able to survive blaming the object more directly. There began to be an amplification of the range of ways of relating that he felt were now possible beyond the performer/audience or cruel parent/ bad baby relationship.

"Where were you?"

A session a couple of months after the one above seemed to demonstrate this. It took place after a Christmas break that was extended because of heavy snow. After telling me he was growing and building up his muscles, and doing some "tough guy" training, he decided that he wanted to play football. There was a problem: we could not find his ball.

> He looked angry about this and went over to the cupboard. He made a kind of monster face and a growling noise. I said I could see he was angry and felt I had really let him down by forgetting his ball. He did angry breathing with a manic smile, and began to tip things out of their boxes and hurl them onto the floor. It felt more purposeful than rage—more like vengeance. I said he was furious with me, but he was pleased as well—it would teach me a lesson and give him a chance to show me what it feels like; I can see what it's like when my stuff is dropped. This caught him, and connected us. I listed my recent failings and all the times through the break and the snow when I had not managed to see him. As I spoke, he knelt on the floor and threw things one by one, first across the room and then more directly at me. I said I thought he wanted me to know he hated me sometimes—it was my fault he had to be so strong, left to cope over Christmas.
>
> He climbed up onto the top of the cupboard and I said no wonder he wanted to be right at the top—king of the castle, because

there was no way he was going to be down there on the floor with all the dropped stuff. I said he felt I didn't care, why should I care? I voiced it from what I felt might be his point of view: "If she cared, she wouldn't have forgotten my ball, she wouldn't have missed any sessions all through Christmas and the snow—she would have got to me somehow".

Sitting tucked up on top of the cupboard looking isolated and small, he said, "Yeah, if she cared she would know what I been through". I said I didn't know what he had been through because I wasn't there. Where was I when he needed me? He said, "Yeah, where were you? You could have helped". I said, "But I didn't. No one came to rescue you. You just had to manage all on your own and you were so little". In a small ordinary voice he talked about how first the court and then mum and dad rescued him. He said it was complicated and I didn't know what had happened. I said it was complicated, and I hadn't been there to help him put it all together. He felt I should have been there, and now all I could do was try to understand.

He began to climb down from the cupboard, and asked me to move the table nearer for him to climb onto. I said he would rather rely on the table to help than me, but not unsympathetically, and he agreed. He talked in a very poignant way about his early life. I felt like crying, and said that it was terribly sad. He talked about having flashbacks at night of when he was a baby, and told me he took it out on his mum when it was not her fault. I said he worried about that, and had been taking it out on me, too, today and it was understandable that he lashed out when I had let him down.

After telling me it was too hot in here and trying to turn the radiator down, he said he wanted to go now. I thought he meant leave the room, but it turned out that he meant an old hiding place of his in the cupboard. He climbed in, as he had not for a long time, wanting the doors to be shut. I could feel tremendous sadness and said that he was on his own in there and he was used to being on his own, and maybe sometimes it felt calmer, but I thought it was important to know that I was outside the door today, thinking about him and waiting for him.

Alongside Dan's fierce longing for togetherness seemed to be a super sensitivity to emotional stimuli. I had tried to put words to some of his painful experiences, and although he did seem to be able to bear this and use it by this stage in our work together, he told me he found it "too hot" and wanted to hide away. To put it another way, I think he struggled with emotional regulation. The intrinsic mind/bodiness of this process is illuminated by Siegel: "The mind's ability to regulate emotional processes is essentially the ability of the brain to modulate the flow of arousal and activation throughout its circuits" (1999, p. 245).

Schore describes how children who have experienced early adversity without much help struggle in "maintaining interpersonal relationships, coping with stressful stimuli, and regulating emotion" (2001, p. 208). Dan was such a child, and I think he may have partly experienced therapy as an ongoing emotional trigger that he needed to protect himself against. He seemed to be using the hiding place as a concrete way of regulating his feelings. He had felt let down, and he had hated me, and after I acknowledged that, we were able to have a moment of contemplating his painful start in life. It was a powerful session, with "hot" material, and he seemed to need to "cool down" by hiding himself away. I was aware of a mental link between us this time, though, which I wanted to highlight in my comment about waiting outside for him and thinking of him. My intention here was to foster the green shoots of a development towards a different internal object relationship that seemed to be under way. He seemed able to be in touch with some sadness, to relinquish the protection of the performance for a little while, in the safety of a relationship that could hold him.

In telling me how his early life was complicated and I did not know what had happened, I think he was beginning to be aware of the psychic taking in, the holding in mind that he had not had. Alvarez's thinking about justice and rectification is significant here. She writes:

> The sense of how things should be is connected, I think, to a deep sense of order, justice, and rightness. When the abused or deprived child indicates a longing for us to adopt him or rescue him, an interpretation along the lines of "You wish but we both know that you can't" may increase despair and weaken the ego. "You feel I should rescue you or you feel somebody should rescue you or you feel your mother should not have abandoned you" may actually strengthen the child so long as it is not done as though containing a promise of actual rescue. (1997, p. 767)

Hindle and Shulman (2008) write about how the absence of this feeling of someone available, a parental holding in mind, can be experienced as a shapeless, meaningless void. This may link with what Dan described as "flashbacks" about his infancy, and the feeling I had in working with him that there was a chasm into which he feared he might fall; for example, the drop between the chair and the table that he had previously stretched across so precariously with his body.

The task of finding some relationship between the different parts of Dan's experience was huge, and the necessary holding together work in sessions, even three times weekly, often felt inadequate and intermittent. The sense of separate worlds and fragmented experience was ongoing. Dan struggled to relinquish for any length of time manic ways of protecting himself from falling apart that were represented by car world and the stuntman. I think he may have experienced sessions as separate worlds sometimes, with no link between them. At other times, he showed me that he was furious with me for not being able to maintain the link; for forgetting to make sure his ball was there, having to finish a session when he needed it to continue, or not preserving the room just as he had left it the session before. However, in the session above, we did seem to have managed to make a connection between us that could tolerate some fierce resentment. This may have helped facilitate a feeling of being taken in that could encompass strong negative feelings without retaliation, as well as positive aspects of him.

Making a den

I would like to turn now to a strand of material integral to the notion of being taken in, involving the making of dens. These had many and various qualities but all seemed to represent a retreat from the pressures of the encounter in the room, a place from which he could interact on his own terms. He wanted to be able to see out, but for me not to be able to see in. I will give material from three key sessions involving dens, which seemed to convey Dan's move from implicit communication towards more explicit acknowledgement between us of emotions, and the beginnings of narrative awareness that could be brought to bear on our relationship.

I. The yo-yo and the volcano

Six months earlier than the "Where were you?" session, he had shown me how, for him, a container turns into a volcano. From inside a den made by a blanket draped over the table:

He was talking in baby language, and I was responding from outside the den. The sound turned into "Yo-yo!" I said yo-yo back. He sat up and said he needed the loo—could he go? I said yes, sure, wondering if it had all got too much, and followed him to stand outside while he went. He carried on talking in yo-yo language in the loo, as if calling to me, and I answered. I had the feeling that he needed to know I was there, and if he didn't hear my voice, he might have thought I had gone. A thought about toing and fro-ing came into my mind in connection with the word yo-yo, and I thought of the comings and goings of our sessions.

Back in the room, I asked if he had thought I might have gone if he didn't hear me. He climbed under the blanket and carried on in yo-yo talk, and I said gently that I thought he needed to know I was there, and that maybe when he couldn't hear someone he thought they'd gone away. Still in the game, in a young voice, he said "Night night", and I said it back. Then in a more ordinary voice, still under the blanket, he said he was making me a pot. I said in a hopeful, interested voice, "Oh, a pot, something to put things in"; then he said, "No, a volcano!" I was struck by the symbolism of this and said, "The pot turns into a volcano!" He got out of the tent, bundled the imaginary pot-volcano into a ball and threw it in the air as if it was burning him. I said, "Ouch! That's burning hot!" He threw it to me and said, "Blow!", which I did. I said the minute there seemed to be somewhere to put things, there was some stuff that felt like a volcano pouring out, burning hot, that needed to be cooled down, and he wanted me to cool it. He held out his hands to have it back, and I said I'd try to throw it slowly so it could cool down. It was still very hot, though, and went to and fro a few times more, getting cooler.

I felt I had a balancing act to do here, where too much linking to feel-ings may have been inflammatory, and yet he was showing me power-ful connections to potentially make more explicit between being cared for and explosive volcanic emotion. The emotion may have been rage, which would fit with the symbolism of the Incredible Hulk material turning up after Spiderman had joined people together. He may also have been communicating a feeling that there was too much hot stuff for any container-person to bear, and they would erupt, just as he often did. Rather than discuss this explicitly, which might have run the risk of escalating his emotion, it seemed necessary to keep it at an implicit body level and do the toing and froing with the idea of the pot representing the hot stuff, cooling down between us.

The problem of containment for his explosive volcanic feelings seemed to have been played out in this material from the early months of the therapy. He conveyed a powerful sense of the improbability of his object having the capacity to take in and contain these forceful feelings. However, after about a year and a half's work, once the "Where were you?" reproach about not having been rescued was taken in by me and became more explicit between us, the quality of the den material in sessions changed somewhat in nature. I will explore the nature of these changes in the following material, taken from a session early in the second year of work, immediately after a session involving a den that he had enjoyed making collaboratively.

II. Rebuilding

On collecting him from the waiting room, he came eagerly towards me and hurried ahead down the corridor. In the room, he smiled conspiratorially and began to move the chair without speaking. He seemed to be busy beginning to reconstruct the den we'd made yesterday. He silently set about gathering the things he needed. He pulled a little table across the room to the cupboard and stood on it, reaching up to throw down Ted and the blankets to me from the top of the cupboard. It was a bit of a challenge to catch them—he threw them away from me as if to make it harder, as he's done when we play catch. I felt he was giving me a test I had to pass—especially in throwing the teddy bear, which I felt I really shouldn't drop. It was a bit of a no-win situation because he seemed disappointed when I didn't drop them, as if I'd won and it made him the loser.

Gesturing with his hand up high and the odd word, he showed me we would need the den to be higher. I said perhaps we needed more room for him today. He used the blankets as a kind of tent as we had done yesterday, and struggled to stick them to the wall and door high enough. Yesterday it was more collaborative, and we had used string to tie things securely, but today he was just using sellotape and trying to do it more on his own. He expressed frustration, again with more hand gestures and facial expressions than words, and asked me to help in a rather exasperated way. I did, but the little bit of sellotape he had cut off to use was straining to hold the weight of the blanket. He listened alertly for the sound of the sellotape unsticking, drew in his breath and said, "Listen!" I said he had to be on the alert for the sellotape unsticking, and alluded to how hard it was to get it to stick today.

He was very keen that paper should cover any gaps between the blankets and furniture that made up the den. He bossed me around quite a bit and seemed irritated. I said I thought perhaps he felt cross with me. The whole process felt much more laborious and frustrating than it did yesterday, and I said that it seemed more of a struggle today; it was the second time we were doing this and it felt a bit different this time. He said accusingly, sounding exasperated: "Because you took it apart!" We had talked about the need for me to do this the day before, but I did not mention that now. I said I thought he was very cross with me about that—he had left it where it was and I had got rid of it after he had gone, and now he had to start again from scratch and it was my fault. With this acknowledgement, the emotional tone changed. He said he wished I had left it, and I was touched and said it was very disappointing for him.

This more muted mood did not last; he carried on working on it for a while, and it got frantic. He climbed around the place, over and under things, in an agile and agitated way to get what he needed, rejecting some things as "no good". He said "Master", and then quickly, "No, helper", and asked me to get him something. I paused before I did what he asked, and said that it seemed like there were two things we could be today—master or helper; someone was in charge and someone did what they said. He said yes. I said I thought he really did not want to be the helper, but he did want to be the master. He said yes, with a winning smile. He carried on working on the den while I sat quietly thinking about him, and he then said crossly that I was not on my break. I began to feel bullied and exhausted, as if there was no rest anywhere. I said perhaps he needed me to know it was exhausting being a helper, you couldn't have a break but had to keep doing what the master said, whether you were tired or not.

Dan's efforts to rebuild the den seemed hampered by his feeling that the safe place we had made the day before had been demolished by me in his absence. His conspiratorial smile at the beginning masked both his disappointment at finding it gone, and his fury with me for having dismantled it, although this burst out later in his "Because you took it apart!", I think this put us on either side of a power divide. We could be master and helper, and he could make a bid for the master role, but we were not felt to be joint co-operators. There was a sense of wariness about how far he felt he could trust me—he wanted to watch me from a place where I could not see him.

> He climbed into the den and shortly afterwards threw a big cushion out. I registered that there was no comfort in this den. He pulled the doll's house across one side of the den, and then said accusingly, "You can see through it". I suggested that it felt really important for him that I could not see in. He had the string with him and asked, more with gestures than words, for help tying it across the legs of the furniture as a kind of fence. He said "Put some paper!" and showed me what he meant—paper strung along the string. I said it looks like you want me to keep out. He told me, "Do a keep out sign", which I did.

There may have been a link here with Bion's bizarre fragments, where the sense organs themselves are felt to contain minutely dissected particles of terrifying unprocessed and unprocessable sensory experience—beta elements (1962, p. 6). Perhaps his sense of my eyes on him was experienced in this way. However, by this stage in the therapeutic relationship, we had weathered a few storms, and it may have been that he wanted to communicate his anger that he felt he could no longer rely on our relationship, now that I had taken apart his den, and wanted to exclude me. If there was an element of something unprocessed, experienced as bizarre fragments, they were now being directed at me as his object, as what he posted out later in the session seems to show:

> I stayed sitting outside by the den and waited, thinking of him inside. He asked if I could see him, and I said no. He said he could see me, and I said maybe he liked it that way round at the moment. It felt more peaceful. He asked if I could see his fingers and he stuck them out and wiggled them about. I smiled and said yes. He asked if I would like him to make funny faces. I wondered aloud if maybe he felt he needed to make funny faces to keep my

interest—it might be hard for him to think I would just sit quietly out here near him, thinking of him, not needing to be entertained. He asked if he was allowed to use the pens. I said sure, thinking he knew that, and wondering whether to comment on it but decided not to for now. He began drawing and said something about doing something rubbish—I said it sounded like he felt what he might make would be rubbish; did it feel like I might think it was rubbish? He said, "No, you won't say it's rubbish."

Here, I was trying to suggest the idea of a different view of things, even if he did not identify with it at that moment. His use of the word "say" instead of "think" may have been a veiled accusation of duplicity— I might think it was rubbish but not say so. I decided not to get embroiled in this possibility, but instead to wait and see what developed.

Then he said, "It's no good!" I registered the "no good" feeling that was around today, and asked, "Why?" He gestured across a little gap in the den with a ruler and said, "That to that!" There was a bit of a pause for a moment as I thought about it, and he said it again. It felt peremptory—as if he was indicating that I should close the gap, and I had not jumped to it quickly enough. Staying where I was, I said there was still a gap and he did not want it. I thought of a letter box, and heard him begin drawing something. Shortly afterwards, he said, "Postage coming in!" and poked his drawing through the gap. It struck me that from his point of view, it was postage going out. I reached over to get it and it was a blue felt tip drawing of a boy with solid legs and a stick—thin tummy. I thought that he did not really have an inside. He was already onto the next sheet of paper, which he said was a newspaper, and he asked how to spell my name. When he pushed it out, I saw that it took the form of an odd assortment of small squares with squiggles underneath them; the kind he'd used before to indicate newspaper writing, and our two names at the side. I was a bit perplexed and held it to think about. As I did so, he said, "No postage—postage needs loo!"

He was angry about my dismantling of the den, and suspicious of my motives in seeing him, but he did seem to want to communicate these feelings rather than hide them. He seems by this stage to have developed a sense of being in relation to someone who did want to understand and be alongside him, however temporarily. The gap, though it still bothered him, seemed to have become something to communicate through, rather than something to fall into. It was an example of our growing attunement that I thought of a letter box, just as he said "postage"—although it was interesting that he said "postage coming in" rather than going out—that is, he was seeing it from my point of view while I was imagining his.

The postage conveyed primitive feelings—the first drawing he posted out to me showed a stick-thin boy with no stomach, no space inside. I think this applied to the room as much as to the boy. Removing the den from the day before may have been experienced as me having got rid of him, having pushed him out of the space I had seemed to be offering for him, leaving him deprived and hungry. The remark "postage coming in" also implies no space for him—it is a role reversal; from his point of view it was going out. He cannot rely on my ability to take in his point of view, but instead accommodates mine, which paradoxically leaves him stick thin. He is not being nourished by a holding mind, the psychic equivalent of the feeding relationship. He is showing me a world in which he has had to do the feeding, which he was inevitably ill-equipped to do. However, the fact that he is showing me this world seems to represent the hope of a different possibility. We are moving away from the dancing waiter who cannot hear any mention of his wait, and who secretes faecal matter into the food. He is able to let me know more directly that he is angry: "Because you took it apart!"

His subsequent postage offering seemed ambivalent; our two names, but in the context of something like a newspaper report. In so far as we did link up together, the resulting connection seemed to be newsworthy, and my hunch was that this may have been for all the wrong reasons. Two people do not normally make the papers for a straightforward warm connection. He did not elaborate on this, though, but he did need to rush to the loo immediately afterwards. This may have been his response to something frightening that was brought up for him by the idea of our two names in the paper.

Back in the room, we only had five minutes left. He got back into his den and carried on with the postage; this time he pushed out a drawing of what looked like a very rudimentary face with two eyes—a round one and a triangular one, a square nose, and a rectangle mouth. There was no outline to the face—just the features, oddly geometric and blank. I found it hard to comment or even form a thought in response, but managed to say something about how he seemed to be giving me something important to think about—it looked rather like a face, but with firm lines instead of soft—apart from one round eye.

Again, Bion's unprocessed fragments spring to mind. Asking him about them drew a blank. It was as if he just needed to hand them to me to think about. It felt primitive, rudimentary—I thought perhaps there was a link with the feeling of frustration and of not wanting to be seen, as if there was something shameful about his delayed development. His heartfelt "It's no good!" earlier in the session seems to apply on several levels: his feeling about his drawings—that they would not be sincerely valued, my failure to cover him up properly, and other shortcomings in me and the therapy, and himself and his efforts generally. My dismantling of the previous day's den seemed to have left him with the feeling that it was all no good, possibly wiping out hopeful feelings that may have emerged before when he seemed to feel we could work together. Yet he was by this stage of the therapy willing and able to communicate that feeling to me—which is quite astonishing given my blindness. I am very aware in writing this that I received the communication without much of a clue; not much processing help for him. However, he may have sensed that I was gamely trying in my own limited way.

It was time to finish and he asked in an in charge kind of way if I would be alright tidying up. As we left, he smiled brightly, and then said, "Bye" to the room and den before we rejoined mum in the waiting room.

In the way he left the room, he seemed to be showing that he was no longer expecting me to preserve the den—keep a space for him. He seemed to have defended himself against both the pain of rejection and the potential destructiveness of anger at my betrayal, as I think he may have experienced it, by resorting to the protection of the role of master/ overseer and assigning me a servile role: "Will you be alright tidying up?" Clearing the den away had become something he was asking me to do, and it felt like revenge—as if he was saying to me: "Oh, you don't care enough to keep the den? This is work to you. I won't care about it either". The fact that he did sometimes feel found by me thus seemed to exacerbate his feeling of trickery on my part—of his having been taken in by something he hoped might be real and lasting, and then turned out to be only fifty minutes of my working day.

There is a conundrum in taking a child into psychotherapy in that the relationship is necessarily close, and feelings about parenting are transferred onto the person of the therapist, but it is a job of work, rather than a personal connection, although that may inevitably grow. Questions about the "real relationship" seem pertinent; after all, I was really in the room, and so was Dan. The qualities of my response to him were particular to me, although there would, I hope, have been overlap between these and the responses of another therapist. Supervision had a vital role here in offering another level of processing of implicit feeling and another world view to contribute to the developing picture. The therapy thus happens in relation to the supervision, rather than entirely in its own little world, so that in parallel with therapy new connections can be made and new possibilities become available. It may have been important that he was able to be in touch with the reality of ending in his "Bye" to the room and the den.

It had begun to be apparent that when it did happen that I as the therapist/object was felt by Dan to respond in a way he could use, and he felt himself to be taken into a relationship he could inhabit, however ambivalently, then it was cruelly taken away all too quickly like the foster placement in which he had begun to settle. The following den material represents this traumatic disruption all too clearly.

III. The "time bomb"

Soon after a week's holiday break towards the end of the second year, he began the session by eagerly showing me a gold award sticker which he said was "good", and then climbed up to stand on a swivel chair. My thinking aloud about whether good stuff like getting a gold award felt risky prompted him to kneel upside down on the spinning chair.

> He began some gymnastic somersaults, but asked me to protect him, which he had never done before. It felt trusting. He tipped over onto a cushion and repeated it several times. Then he said he wanted to make a den, explaining that it wasn't about being angry today—a reference to yesterday's den—it was a different sort of den.

This time the process felt mostly collaborative. As usual, he wanted to make sure no light could get in, and soon began ordering me about in a rather tyrannical way. However, by now we could have conversations about what things felt like, that did not trigger him, if I managed to talk in a way he could tolerate. He let me know that not having the light shining in seemed to be about being able to rest, without the spotlight glare of my attention. This seemed to link with his need to turn a desk light on me sometimes, reversing the inquisition that he felt therapy to be. Having constructed the den:

> He sat inside and I waited outside. After a minute, he invited me to join him. I was surprised, and cautiously wondered aloud first whether there might be a feeling that he had to entertain me to stop me going away, which he denied. However, it did also feel like a big step for him, inviting me to join him where he was, and so I said thank you, and came in and sat down. He got the tea set out and I wondered tentatively aloud whether we were seeing the waiter coming out. He smiled and said, "No, let's have a cup of tea", which felt more companionable, albeit on his terms. However, after a little while of this companionable being together feeling, we were back in the cafe and he was the cafe owner offering sausage and chips—he said it was a big sausage. I said maybe he thought I was the kind of person who would only be interested in a big sausage, not a little one, and he agreed. As he sorted out plates and cups and food, I added that maybe he was wondering what he needed to do to keep me interested in him, maybe just sitting here together did not feel like enough—I wondered what he thought might happen if he didn't feed me.
>
> He made no reply, and gathered up the tea things as if he had something else in mind. Feeling cruel, but not wanting the ending to be a shock, I said I needed to keep an eye on the time. It was five minutes till the end, and I let him know that. He got up and crashed through the den walls, breaking it up. I said it felt horrible; it was a shock, ending so quickly. He said it was a time bomb. I said just when he was starting to feel someone was with him and there was something good, time was up and it felt like I had set a time bomb—I was chucking him out and everything was destroyed. He hurled himself onto the armchair head first to tumble over it like before, but I was not there this time to protect him, and he hit his

leg on the side of the chair. I said it hurt him and I had not been there to catch him.

For Dan, then, endings felt like time bombs. He seemed to feel lured into a cruel trap I had set whereby I was in control of the timing of the ending, and was only pretending to be fully with him while really I was getting ready to kick him out if he did not feed me. I think this may have been his unconscious feeling about not only therapy but his experience of the families he had lived with too. There seemed to be a question around, something like: can it be good if it ends? Or perhaps, can it be real if it ends, or does that make it a cruel trick?

I think the balance of delight and deception in being taken in here was a difficult one, and I thought in supervision about the way in which I was being taken into his den. My feeling was of an invitation into his space, which had an element of something delightful and potentially real, though laced with something less in touch with the reality of time and endings and so perhaps deceptive too.

Along with the external disruption of the imminent ending of the session, there was also a sense that any companionable feelings were quickly disturbed by an internal relationship in which he was not to be "fed" something of value by someone else. He was to do the feeding, as in the waiter/chef material. To further complicate matters, intertwined in this material are likely to be qualities of the potentially rivalrous relationships between his birth mother, grandmother, and other carers, internalised in his early years as his developing mind made connections. Inevitably, then, the process of trying to "feed" him my attempts to understand him was itself suspect rather than neutral. He seems to have experienced it as an attempt to take him in as a confidence trick. However, we were able by this stage to think explicitly about the process of our relationship as he experienced it—for example, what might happen if he didn't feed me, or the feeling that I had set a time bomb that would destroy everything—without it triggering rages or manic behaviour, or a need to get out of the room. It did cause him pain, though, as he showed in hurling himself over the chair and hurting himself when I was not there to catch him.

My not being there, not finding him when he was hurt and needed me, links to the theme of hide and seek, which as I mentioned in the introduction was an important strand of the clinical material.

Hide and seek

Dan seemed in this game to be conveying many things, one of which was a wish to be found by me in the way a mother finds her baby. He would speak poignantly about wanting me to close my eyes and find him by feeling, not seeing. Tellingly, though, this eventually turned into a game in which I was made to look ridiculous, to his huge amusement. He was showing me an internal world in which somebody looking for someone else—somebody needy—is inevitably made to look a fool and mocked, and that was certainly not going to be him.

In the series of three sessions I now offer for consideration, Dan communicated through this game the extreme nature of his experience of neglect. Taken together, the three excerpts that follow seem to represent a shift. The unprocessed, fragmentary, rather bizarre and confusing feeling, which to begin with ran implicitly under the "You say wow!" element, seems to have surfaced, and is now directed to me for a processing function. Like the geometric face elements posted out from the den, it seemed that some of this feeling had now begun to arise in a way that he felt could be attended to in our relationship.

I. The survivor

This session occurred after a half term break when we had worked together just over two years. It started with him stumbling headlong down the corridor into the room.

> In the room, he plonked himself down in the easy chair, sighed, and visibly relaxed. "Made it!" he said. I said, "You finally got here, looks like it was quite an effort". He said yeah, and swung his legs, kicking each one out in turn and saying, "Oooh!" quietly, as if it hurt. I asked if his legs were hurting, and coming over to sit on the desk beside me, he said he had had PE yesterday, then street dance, then more dancing till half past eight. I said it sounded like his muscles had been really stretched with all that activity, and that we thought about his mind and feelings too here, and that maybe it's been quite an effort, quite a stretch waiting to come here again—to hold on all that time, all through half term. He said yeah, it was.

He then painted a scene involving a house and some fog, and some wild animals behind a fence, all of which seemed heavy with symbolism connected to the difficulty of finding his object again and the need to fend off wild feelings about absence. Then:

> He stood by the door and noticed the lock, saying he'd never seen that before. He turned it, and I said that was the two of us locked in now. He said he wasn't going anywhere, and I said it looked like I wasn't either; he said, "No one can get in". It felt as if he might be saying we are protected from danger in here. I said no one could get in but I couldn't get out either; we would just have to stay here— just him and me. Maybe that was the only way he could be sure of me, to be in the same room—hard to imagine I could keep him in mind even when we weren't in the same room. He smiled and unlocked it, then jumped onto the swivel chair and stretched his arms out saying he needed me to pull him along.

His comment about his not going anywhere seemed to echo what I had said during the earlier Spiderman material when he had sellotaped me to the chair: that it looked like I wasn't going anywhere. He had loved this remark, and often referred to it over the years. I felt that locking the door here, albeit temporarily, was his way of making a claim on me as his object. It felt developmental—he was prepared to acknowledge that there was a relationship he wanted to hang onto in spite of its temporary nature and the coming and going of sessions with painful breaks when I was not there to "pull him along".

> I pulled him along on the chair for the length of the room, and then I said I was going to sit down and think about him. He said he was left to manage on his own now, and started what sounded like a film commentary about a tropical storm, huge waves, and a survivor. He managed to pull himself on top of the cupboard, and I said the survivor was up high now, out of the waves, safer but all alone. He grabbed Ted and cuddled him tight, saying he was a little boy he'd rescued. He tipped forward and almost fell—he quickly had to jump down, but landed on his feet. I think it gave him a shock and I said so, and that I needed to be nearer when he was up high like that. I stood by as he climbed up again and tipped towards the edge, ready for me to catch him. I said he had nearly fallen and it was a horrid shock, and this time he wanted me to catch him—there was nothing worse than falling with no one to catch you. Maybe half term had felt like I'd dropped him. He did actually tip off the edge of the cupboard, cuddling Ted, and I carried him to the chair.

Then he initiated a game of hide and seek:

> In a baby voice, he said, "Has and deek", which he then repeated
> as hide and seek. I said he really wanted me to find him, especially
> after the long half term break where he felt I hadn't found him,
> had let him drop, and he felt alone and frightened like the survivor
> in the big tropical storm. He asked me to count long enough for
> him to hide, and I counted slowly to twenty. At first he hid behind
> the chair where I could easily find him. I said the survivor really
> wanted to be found after all he'd been through. He wanted to play
> again, and hid twice on top of the cupboard under a blanket. After
> the third time we had to finish, and I said I would find him again
> on Thursday, and it might be hard for him to think that I would
> keep him in mind till then, but it was time to finish and go back to
> mum for now.

This session material was in some ways surprising, coming as it did
after a break. He showed a vulnerability that was often hidden in sessions, and a capacity to symbolise that put him at one remove from the
experience of being dropped. On this occasion, he was able to play it
out imaginatively and represent it in painting, rather than physically
attack me as retribution for my absence, or run out of the room. He
included an identification with a helpful figure who could notice and
respond to need in his rescue of Ted. It felt like an extension of his rep-
ertoire of ways of being together.

However, the very next session felt quite different, and I include it
to illustrate how fleeting was the presence of the helpful figure in his
internal world. This figure soon becomes suspicious, even monstrous,
and was strikingly hard to include in our verbal communications.

II. Turning into a monster

He was eager to start this session, wanting to play hide and seek
immediately. He did not want me to delay by talking at all—it felt like
there was not a moment to lose.

> I said it felt urgent; he didn't want to wait for me to do any think-
> ing or talking. He told me to count, and crawled behind my chair
> and tried to get right underneath it. It felt very young and primi-
> tive, as if he wanted to hatch out from under me. He kept very still

and seemed to want me to look for him all round the room before finding him, seeming to be held by the search. I found him and he was delighted, and immediately wanted to play again, telling me not to look while I counted to twenty.

This time he tried to hide out of sight, unlike last session, so that even when I was looking I wouldn't be able to find him. When I found him, he looked a bit hunted and uncomfortable, and said he had been trying to get his feet out of sight. I commented on the "out of sight"—it felt like the mood had changed; perhaps it wasn't such a nice feeling now, being found. I talked about how he'd had to hold an uncomfortable position that was hard to stay in, and wondered how it felt when I was looking for him this time. He did not want to talk about this or anything else, insisting on getting on with another game of hide and seek as quickly as possible. As he looked for somewhere to hide, he showed me how he'd come out from behind the blind and then leapt off the desk while I was counting. The implication was how stupid I had been not to realise he was leaping around. He told me to count again—even more slowly this time. We played this a few more times, and I felt desperation in his voice and manner as he looked for somewhere to hide. I asked what it felt like while I was counting. He made a panicky face to show me, and I said there seemed to be something frightening now, something panicky about someone coming to look for him; I thought perhaps he felt I'd turned into a monster coming to get him. He didn't want me to talk about it, and I said I thought maybe he felt even talking about it might be too hard at the moment.

He got his paints and brush and took them over to the desk. He twirled the brush in the black and I waited to see what he was showing me. He brought it over and stirred it into a jug of water by my side, and then did the same with each of the other colours, making a cloudy mixture. It took quite a while, and I waited and watched while he did this, and then he said those were his feelings. I said how cloudy they were, all mixed up and confused and hard to see through. We talked about all the colours that had gone in, first the black and then grey and then all the other brighter ones. I noticed that he'd started with the dark ones, and they had coloured all the other colour feelings that had gone in there, and now they were all muddled together. Perhaps he was showing me he felt confused, with all those feelings in a murky cloud, and that the dark colours made everything dark.

He got his little football out of his box and began to paint colours on it. First black, because he said a real football was muddy, and I said yes—if you use a real football it does get muddy, and perhaps there's a real muddy, messy part of you that you're showing me too. He got yellow on his brush and painted a section yellow, and I asked about yellow—what it reminded him of. He smiled and said it was like wee. I said there was wee on this feelings ball, as well as the mucky stuff. He then painted some red on it, saying, "Arsenal!" I said, "Arsenal?" He said, "Yeah, they're great", and I talked about how they were a great football team—kind of champions. I said I thought he wanted some winning feelings on there; when he thought of mud and wee kind of feelings I thought it made him want to think about champion feelings, to get away from all that mess maybe. He painted blue on there too, and said it was like the sky. I talked about it as something beautiful in the mix too, and said how I thought that painting the ball was showing us something very important about him—the dark difficult feelings he has, like when he feels frightened and needs to keep out of sight the wee feelings, and the wanting to be a winner feelings, and the beautiful blue feelings—all those different feelings, all part of him, and how they all seemed to get mixed up together sometimes.

Although the words here do seem to relate to what he was showing me on one level, it felt a bit pat. Interestingly, the ending of this session left me with some difficult feelings. Rather like the very early waiter session I have included in which I felt that what I said was aimed at an older part of him, here again there was something much more primitive under the surface. I felt that everything had gone wrong; that I had not managed to make it all right as he needed me to, and so he felt the need to attack. I felt that he wanted me to prevent attacks so that he did not have to, and that I had failed in this. It occurred to me that there might be a link with the fenced off wild animals in the painting he did before playing hide and seek last session.

Even though we touched on the feeling that I seemed to represent something monstrous to him during the second hide and seek phase, perhaps this feeling was felt to be too dangerous to really explore, and so it was left with me as an emotional communication. He moved on to show me how confusing it all was by mixing up the colours in the water jug, and maybe by this stage in the therapy, a little way into our second year, he had internalised an expectation that feelings could be represented and thought about, not just acted out. This is particularly striking, given the extreme nature of his fears to do with absence, which seemed to be a matter of life and death. Perhaps this is why the emotional impact of it stayed with me at the end of the session—maybe fears about absence, and about the damage his consequent anger could do was the real communication. Indeed, his early neglect was extreme, and could have meant starvation. Maybe the water jug was just to muddy the waters, letting me think I had made a useful contribution about the colours when in fact he was clouding the issue of his anger. As he might experience it: how could I go, when I knew he would starve? The hide and seek material seems to suggest an implicit feeling of wanting to be found, then fears about this monstrous person (who had cruelly gone in spite of his need of her) finding him again. We managed to touch on this between us, in his showing me the panic he felt as I searched for him, but this was soon succeeded by the water jug material, which felt as though it rather concealed than expressed deeper feelings.

The third phase of the hide and seek game demonstrated this all too clearly. I offer some material from a session that took place two weeks after the previous two excerpts, to further investigate this process. Between this next session and the one before, there had been another two missed sessions.

III. Dead man walking

He seemed anxious when I collected him, and after some worries about whether I was alright, he picked up his football and turned it around in his hands, looking it over, and I watched for a while. "Maybe you're wondering if it's alright too", I suggested …"the Dan-ball with all your feelings. It's been a while since we met—we've missed two sessions". Having kicked it against the door, he said, "Come on—let's play hide and seek!" He said he was going to "do a weird place". A weird place, I registered. "Come on!" he said. I said OK, and started counting. "Count slowly!" he told me imperiously, which I did.

He hid tucked in behind my chair, crouching in the bin. When I found him right behind me, I talked about how it looked like he wanted closeness at the moment, but there was something difficult about it—he was in the bin—perhaps he felt rubbish, or thrown away? No, he said, climbing out, it was just a hiding place—he did say it was going to be a weird place. I told him it made me think of the cool guy/weird guy picture he'd done a while ago—maybe he sometimes felt there was something weird about him that deserved to be in the bin. He told me he was going to do another weird place this time—I was to count very slowly again. This time he was under some big floor cushions, with his back showing. I said it seemed like a comfier place than the bin, and part of him was showing. Maybe this was somewhere the part of him that felt weird could find a place and be seen. He wanted to hide again, and this time he lay along the radiator shelf, partly under the edge of the desk, but most of him easy to see, with his arm hanging down and his eyes shut. I thought he looked like a dead person, and also that it must hurt—it was a squash to get under the desk. He struggled out with a smile when I found him, saying it didn't hurt. I said that there was a big smile, but underneath there seemed to be something quite difficult going on. I thought he might be feeling pretty weird and rubbish today—perhaps there was a link with the two missed sessions? No, he said, it was not my fault; that was because mum was ill. I said mum's ill; maybe there's a worry that you may have hurt her—the way he seemed to hear this made me think I could go further—perhaps you feel too weird for her to manage, and feel you deserve hurting today.

On re-reading this as part of a series with the previous two hide and seek sessions, it seems to me to represent the development of a capacity to reflect together on the qualities of what was happening in the room, rather than just act it out between us. He seems by this stage in the work to be less triggered by my seeing him, and my thinking about what he was showing me. It was possible for us to begin to make the implicit qualities of his communication more explicit between us.

After these reflections, though, there followed a rather conflicted period, when he did not seem to know quite what to do with himself or how to use me or the toys. For example, he got the tea set and then the petrol station out, and stood holding them as if not sure what to do with them—use them or throw them. He seemed to feel at a loss, as if he had an idea that some filling up, some nourishment, might be available, but he was not at all sure about it. He climbed on top of the cupboard, where he tended to go when he was feeling small, and then climbed down again. His mood was slower and more hesitant, not as manic as it had been at similar times in the past. Then the energy levels ramped up, and he pushed himself to and fro on the swivel chair between me and the wall, faster and faster.

> He came back towards me with his hands outstretched for me to catch him. As he hurtled to and fro, he said it was a skeleton. I asked what he meant and he said, "You know, skeleton bobsleigh". I registered something else dead and asked what happens in that. He said it whizzes along very fast and wins. I wondered about this, and watched him carrying on whizzing to and fro, bashing into the walls and furniture. As he came towards me quite fast, I felt as if he'd have half liked to sit on my lap and half liked to bash against me. I said maybe he didn't know if he wanted me to catch him or wanted to bash into me.

There was certainly something around in this session to do with death. It felt as if it was on the verge of becoming explicit, having first been acted out in a dead body hide and seek position along the radiator— there may have been a link with times he has felt things to be "too hot" in the room. He then referred to it in the skeleton bobsleigh, which hurtles down steep icy slopes—too cold. It seemed to be connected with the feeling of weirdness he had shown me initially, and with the feeling of ambivalence that seemed so much in evidence in this session, represented symbolically by the following material:

> He got down and handed me the sellotape to hold. He got the string and cut a long length. He asked me to stick it to the desk, and stuck the other end on top of the cupboard. He sat up there and held one end, then told me to take the desk end and pull for a tug of war. I said it felt like a real struggle today, maybe he felt pulled two different ways.
>
> Then he got down and said he wanted to make a big den, and I said maybe the struggle felt too much just now—he needed a den. As he made it, he wanted it darker, asking me to make sure the blankets spread as far as possible to block out the light. He also wanted it bigger so that he had more room inside. He took some paper and his box in with him—the reason why turned out to be so that I wouldn't have anything else to do: "You're just waiting to see

outside". I said I was not to get interested in anything else while he was in there, he just needed me to watch and wait for him.

He drew something with felt pen and passed it out, saying, "Postage coming!" I thought that he hadn't done this for ages. On the page was a phallic shape, and inside it, a man shooting a gun towards a stick-man dead on the ground. He told me the man has killed someone, and told me to pass it in. I passed it to him, saying he was showing me something very serious, the man had killed someone. I wasn't sure how best to take this up, but was aware that he seemed to be more interested in the killer than the victim at this point. I was conscious that the session was coming to an end. Inside the den he got on with something I couldn't see, and told me I didn't know what he was doing. I said I just had to wait and see, without knowing what was going on. He had drawn the face "of the shooting man" in a circle and then rubbed green Play-Doh on it. I wondered aloud if he was showing us both that the shooting had something to do with the "yucky stuff".

This session material seemed to link a number of key themes: hide and seek, a feeling of unacceptability expressed in his feeling of weirdness, the den, and something ambivalent to do with a kind of winning that seemed to be life and death. There was a figure emerging as the killer, linked with crime scene material. The figure of the killer was shadowy, although he had drawn a face to represent him. I think there may have been a shadowiness about him because Dan himself was not too clear who was responsible for the killing. He had represented himself as the victim in his "dead body" hiding place early in the session, as if neglect had killed him; in which case, I as his object was the killer. However, smearing the figure with green Play-Doh suggested the nappy "yucky stuff", and implied that the guilty party may have been felt to be the "bad baby". The identity of the victim was not clear either. Later material suggested that he felt a tremendous weight of guilt for having left his birth family behind, as if they had had to be killed off in order for him to have a different life. I elaborate this material in order to demonstrate the complexity of his ambivalence about being taken in in being adopted, and taken into psychotherapy, which he felt was "pulling him along" towards something new, and thus inevitably leaving something behind.

Stuntgirl, the "murderator", and the empty house

Since the very beginning we have seen how the presence of a show seemed central for Dan. The darker themes behind the show gradually emerged as the work continued, and our relationship was felt to be able to face pain and cruelty as well as delight. A session that happened soon after his eleventh birthday highlighted the feeling of cruel deprivation behind the show, and an associated wish for murderous revenge.

He straight away went for the motorbikes, saying, "There's going to be a show". He spotted a car with missing wheels and mentioned it, glancing at me now and again with a little smile. He seemed controlled; it felt premeditated and rather ominous as he set up the stage. The motorbikes usually meant car world. I was aware that he had had his birthday at the weekend; it had been a very big deal in the run-up, and I wondered what was in his mind. He rummaged through the box of figures, and muttered that the girl was missing. He quickly picked up another girl figure and dismissed the problem of the missing girl. I said he was hurrying on, but things did seem to be missing today—first the wheels and now the girl. He hurriedly got on with the show, trying to distract my attention. I said maybe he was showing me he felt he just had to move on very quickly and not notice when something was missing.

Engrossed with the figures, he talked in the girl's voice about being afraid to do stunts. A firm voice answered her: "You have to do it anyway". Her worries about doing it without her mummy or head protection or practice were disregarded. I said he seemed to be showing me a world that was very frightening for children; where they had to manage without protection, there was no choice. The girl had to do a daring jump anyway—off the end of the table. She did survive, but she hated it and was very angry and protested.

I said she hated being made to do such dangerous things and was furious about it. I added that I wondered too if perhaps he was showing me something about being here—after his birthday, and what it felt like to him. I could feel trepidation and added that perhaps there was something scary or missing for him. He talked over me as I said this, and seemed to hate me for it. I said we seemed to be out of touch today—he wanted me to just watch the performance, but it was a way of us not really getting together. I said I felt

there was something really bothering him, but whatever it was he
didn't want me to notice.

The stunts got more and more daring. He constructed a series of
ramps, saying it was the murderator, and put the girl on it. I was
shocked—it seemed cruel. I said it looked like a stunt but it was
actually deadly—she could be murdered. He made her skate down,
and manage it, but it was a superpower "car world" kind of man-
aging. He made her leap high in the air and twist round against the
wall, dropping vertically to land on the floor unharmed.

I think the "murderator" was the focus for a whole constellation of
external and internal feelings and relationships. It seemed to me that
the stuntgirl might stand for a more vulnerable part of him, forced by
me in the transference to perform terrifying feats in leaping over deadly
drops between sessions without head protection. I think it likely that a
part of him would have liked me to be the girl on the murderator, too,
getting a taste of my own medicine. Although the girl's safe landing
was not entirely convincing, she was spared death on the murderator.
Perhaps at some level he did feel, too, that the more tender parts of him
would survive our relationship.

Other stunts followed, involving jumping over emergency vehicles
with the fire engine ladder extended to make it harder. My remarks
about jumping over something that's normally there to rescue people were ignored, and again, I think, felt to be infuriating. He dan-
gled the petrol station from the end of the fire engine ladder—it felt
horrible. I said he was making sure nothing was going to be filled
up from that petrol station. I felt the same thing was happening
between us, and tried to put that into words—not only his lack of
expectation that someone would be able to help, but his active pre-
vention of that happening.

Looking back, the point seems to have been that I was to notice that I
did not notice what I was putting him through. Had I clearly apprehended this at the time, the problem of how to communicate it in the
session would have arisen. In terms of the central theme of being taken
in, it raises the question of how to take in the feeling of not having
been taken in; or rather, having been taken in and then dropped, and
exposed to extreme risk.

As the session went on, I felt more and more hopeless and silenced. I couldn't find a way of talking to him about it that was the least bit helpful. My attempts seemed to escalate the feeling of cold cruel danger.

There followed a chaotically confused and confusing series of events in which it was hard to know who was who. Police were involved, children had to persuade unreliable adults to give them a home, and once in the house, the girl hung upside down on her bike from the roof. I said it was a very cruel upside down mixed—up world he was showing us, where you couldn't rely on anyone to help and children could be killed. He said with a grim satisfaction, yes, it was his world.

Then he brought over the fire engine with its ladder up, and got the policewoman to climb it. I felt relief, and the possibility of some sort of order, but also concern about an inspection that could be judgemental. She got into the house, followed by a policeman, and said it was an empty house. This felt very bleak, and coming right at the end of the session made it feel even bleaker.

It seems that behind the show and the extreme cruelty of the murderator was the bleak empty house, which links with the idea of something missing from the beginning of the session. He was showing us both a world in which children could be killed, which links with the death material in earlier sessions. My difficulty in reaching him in this world, which he said was his world, is apparent in the session material, and was perhaps illustrated by the policewoman climbing such a long ladder into the house, but it was very hard to think about while it was happening. I felt that anything I said, or even thought, exacerbated the feeling of cruelty—as if my attempts to understand were part of the problem for him, and the show was his protection. I realised and said that he seemed to be showing me a frightening world where children had to manage without head protection, but did not fully link it to his relationship with me, which seemed to put him in just that situation. In fact he used the symbol of a climber with no ropes in a sequence of play after a year's therapy to show just how deadly was the drop between sessions. My dilemma, so often in working with Dan, was that keeping my comments in the play seemed to avoid responsibility for the situation in the room, but mentioning this directly felt inflammatory. I think he wanted to communicate the feeling that no one was there to help with the appalling cruelty, and so my efforts to notice and help were profoundly frustrating—maddening, even. Perhaps there is a link with his cry right at the beginning in response to my attempts to name the desperation: "No—the lady can't see it!" Any help I did give was taken away all too quickly—and destroyed by the "time bomb". He was not going to subject himself to that risk, but would instead subject the petrol station to dangerous dangling, so that it could not fill anything up.

Furthermore, given that this session took place just after his birthday, I think the bleak emptiness and sense of something missing may once again have been focused around my representation of the missing and neglectful birth mother in not being present. Perhaps he was wrestling internally, on the cusp of Bion's development: "Sooner or later the 'wanted' breast is felt as an 'idea of a breast missing' and not as a bad breast present" (1962, p. 34). But the extremity of his early experience, coupled with his fury, seems to have been too much for him and tipped him towards the persecutory end of this spectrum. If so, this would have made me both perpetrator and inspector—no wonder he was not amenable to hearing what I had to say.

The feeling of my badness, though frightening, may have been better for his development than the "bad baby" identification, in that at least I was held to be the source of the problem. However, this would make my attempts to understand feel cruel in that he may have experienced them as like a police investigation designed to expose his emptiness and subject him to the feeling of bleakness, something like rubbing a dog's nose in its mess—when it was actually my fault.

Being taken in: the abandoned dog and the show

In what he said was his world, the exposure of need was followed by cruelty rather than hope of rescue. Returning to the idea of rescue that was explicitly introduced in the "Where were you?" session, and linking it to the need for a cover-up "show", I would now like to turn to Dan's use of a dog motif. There was a little soft toy dog in the box of play materials I had provided for him, and this dog would often be thrown and kicked around in sessions. It seemed to represent the kicked around part of him, with which he would not explicitly identify. This was understandable if in his world need evoked cruel responses. If there was any kicking around, he wanted to be on the kicking side, not the kicked. I once to my shame inadvertently called him by his family dog's name, which is similar to his own. I thought of the sharp pang of shame as mine, but then wondered if I may also have been picking up on his non-verbal cues. Perhaps it related to the "remarkable thing" (Freud, 1915d) of unconscious-to-unconscious communication that we might now call empathy. This is substantiated in Schore's (2003) right-brain-to-right-brain channel of communication, allowing us to feel undercurrents of feeling running below the words.

In a session some way into the second year of the work, he used the symbol of a dog to convey some powerful feelings of hurt and abandonment, and, for the first time, the dawning hope of a sustained compassionate response.

> I was a few minutes late to collect him from the waiting room, and on arriving in the therapy room he told me Thursday was going to be a sad day; his dog was "getting it cut off". I thought of Dan's own emerging manliness. I asked why, and he said he was humping everything. Very soon, he started to tell me about a sad abandoned dog that he'd seen in a hot country, and how he dreamt about him and wanted to go and rescue him. I wondered aloud if the two dogs might be linked in his mind, the one that humps everything, and the one that is abandoned. I said it might be a bit like how I was late, just when he was wanting to see me.
>
> We talked for some time about the pain of the abandoned dog, until Dan shook his head and said not to talk about him any more. "Too painful and sad?" I asked, and he said yes, he hated to think of it. I agreed that it was very painful to think about; maybe he needed me to just keep it in my mind? He said yes, but went back to the subject, and the practicalities of taking care of him. This felt like something new in our sessions, and I was heartened. He pictured himself, first alone when he was older, and then with mum and dad as back-up, going to rescue him and any other dogs who were abandoned, and give them a home and proper food. He said not to talk about it any more. There was a pause, and then he said, "but I think about him at night". We said nothing for a moment, and I felt we were both picturing the poor dog, and feeling the sadness of it. He said he had barbed wire marks on him. I thought of the hurt abandoned dog in Dan, and said he felt the marks of cruelty on him were still there.

He took out a picture from last session in which he was lead singer in a stadium performance, and added the dog high in the air above the stage. I thought of going from abandoned to on high—zero to hero, as it were. It reminded me of his performances, and of his practising this week for a theatre company show.

We seemed by this stage in the work to be able to feel the sadness of the abandoned dog together, although it was painful, and talk about my disappointing him in a more regulated and less explosive way. His attempts to celebrate the dog in a compensatory way may have had something of the superhero about it, placing him up there above the stage. However, the dog was suspended from a wire rather than represented as supernaturally flying, and the stage felt a very different place from car world and the murderator—particularly as Dan is genuinely a talented performer.

He knelt right by me as we worked on the picture, and it felt quite close in a companionable way. He added a Superman cape to the dog. I said, "Do you think he wants to feel really special like Superman, to make up for feeling so low?" He made a "maybe" face. "What does it feel like for him up there above the others?", I wondered. "He likes it up there", he told me. I suggested that maybe it was pretty exciting up there, but I wondered where he went when he wanted a bit of calm. He said, "On the toilet with the paper". I thought of an identification with his father and of his early remark about getting it cut off, and said, "Hmm, a bit like dad?" and Dan said yeah. Thinking of him alone in there like he used to be in his hiding place in the cupboard, I added that maybe it was hard for him to find a calm place when other people were around; maybe it sometimes felt like he was either performing, or else he had to go to the toilet to get rid of stuff and be on his own.

He moved away to work on his own, and said, "Don't be offended". I said he was worried that I'd be hurt if he moved away to be on his own, and talked about this calmer on-your-own feeling. I mentioned a big eye that he had drawn behind the stage: "Someone's eye is on you—mine?", I asked, and wondered how it felt being watched. He said it was good and bad. This had the feeling of a mixture, rather than the maddening chaos of earlier sessions.

He got the shared felt pens that he preferred to the ones in his box. They usually carried overtones of disappointment and resentment because I had not bought him any for his box, even though I know he would have liked me to. He gave me a look of silent reproach, which I took. Then he found an old stormy lightning picture of his as the template for drawing a zigzag Easter egg, which he wanted to be a joint effort between us, not just him.

The dog motif in this session seemed to be used to exemplify first the cruel neglect, then a dawning sense of hope of a compassionate response. After thinking about the isolation of the show, which had been his way of countering the neglect, there seemed to come a more real sense of wanting something mutually created, which brought joyful possibilities—the Easter egg with its transformed stormy patterns. This seemed to represent a growing capacity for emotional regulation—his wild stormy feelings could be survived between us, and so were less terrifying in his own mind; they had not destroyed everything in their wake. There was the potential for something new between us in his mental landscape, represented by the Easter egg. My role seemed to be more background than foreground now:

> I wondered in my own mind how active my part in the Easter egg drawing would need to be, but it became clear that my job was to be nearby and take an interest. He sat back proudly looking at the egg he had drawn, and the idea of chicks hatching came to mind. I could feel that it looked beautiful to both of us, even radiant. I said how beautiful it was, and added something about new life coming out of eggs. I asked if he felt proud of it. He told me that he didn't feel especially proud because it was just natural to him, but in my mind it was something to be proud of.

I felt touched that he was acknowledging the world of our relationship in which I would be proud of what he did, rather than still living in a world in which what he did was not valued, as in some of the earlier postage material, which he felt was rubbish.

The progress we had made between us in emotional regulation, represented by the egg with its transformed stormy patterns, seemed to be consolidated a month later when I had been delayed getting to a session immediately after a week's break. As we have seen, my not being there had triggered life and death anxieties in previous stages of the therapy, and there was still a worry that this might happen:

> Although he was agitated and wanted me to be quiet in case things got ruined, he was able to let me say very gently that although he didn't like me talking about it, I thought it would be good if I could ask what needed to happen. He paused and looked at me—half reproachfully, half hopefully. "Should I have tried harder to get to you quicker?" I asked. He said yes, in a resolved way, and it seemed to give him some relief. He then drew what he said was "a quiet volcano" with smoke instead of lava and said it was erupting. I said he was angry and upset, but it did not seem to be ruining everything this time. The final effect of the drawing was rather fragmented, but there was a defined landscape, with features other than the volcano.

In the earliest stages of the work, as we have seen, I was unable to put into words much of the complexity of feeling evoked in sessions. Following Stern (2004), it may be that this was an essential part of the repair work of the therapy, and meant that we were more in the present moment together than if I had too quickly stepped outside it for the third-person perspective. In Klein's (1935) terms, it may have meant that I was felt to be more able to survive his attacks on me. Perhaps the lack of the immediate protection of a carapace of understanding helped him feel sometimes that I had emotionally taken in the full force of what he was giving me. This early stage of implicit communication seems to have laid the foundations for later work in which the relationship could begin to endure feelings of exposure or exclusion evoked by the third perspective of the explicit apprehension of feeling states. We could reflect together on our relationship, and could acknowledge my disappointing him without destructive eruption. There was still an emotional volcano, but it was "a quiet volcano" with smoke instead of lava, and room for other things in the landscape.

"I wanted to give you a heart attack"

After three years of work, we had scaled down to twice weekly sessions because he was now in secondary school with the first term under his belt, and didn't want to miss his favourite subject, games, which clashed with our third session. After three months of this phase of weaning, for similar reasons, we were due to reduce to once weekly sessions for the final term. I would not say that he had entirely internalised a capacity for emotional regulation; indeed, sometimes it felt as though no progress had been made.

One session around this time, for example, began with him throwing things at me then laying across my chair, feeling very cold and lonely but not able to take any comfort. I felt desolate myself, as if it was all in vain and we were back to square one. Noticing this, I thought it might be a communication about how Dan was feeling too:

> I said that he went to a dark dead place when I didn't come and get him; where it all felt hopeless, and he felt I'd been cruel. He laughed in a cruel way, and went towards the door. I felt desperately sad as if it was all no use. I did not think he could hear about this sad feeling in his present state of mind. I decided it would be more productive to take up the feeling of cruelty in relation to what he may have felt I was feeling. I said he felt I was laughing at him somewhere else, knowing he needed me but not caring, and laughing at his hurt. I said I thought it made him feel he had got to get his own back and be cruel too, to give me a taste of my own medicine. "Yes!" he said vehemently, and came over to crouch behind my chair.

After nearly four hundred hours of trying to tune into his states of mind and feeling, the difference at this later stage seemed to be that he hoped I might be able to do it, and was prepared to let me try. His world view seemed now to include a relationship in which someone would make this attempt, and might sometimes succeed in resonating with and naming his emotional experience, so that it was a joint process, rather than entirely his alone to bear. In the face of the cruelty we were talking about and feeling, he crouched behind my chair, which seemed to offer him some sort of protection.

The last session before we reduced to once weekly sessions for the last term of therapy was a kind of rehearsal of ending altogether. Rather than triggering a retreat into old patterns, there seemed to be a new development:

> He talked about a drumming group he was in, four of them together, which sounded like a development, but also felt staged— like a cover story for drumming to block me out, which he then did.

I talked about how this was good news but might also be a cover story, a smoke screen for a deeper feeling. I said I thought he feared I might mess it up by talking about his feelings and winding him up so that the last session was spoiled. He said, "I'll hurt you if you don't do what I say." I said I felt this was not so much a threat as a worry, and then said there was a question, "Is this a world where that's how we are together?" He visibly slackened and said slowly that this was a world about "care—love—cuddles" that he now had with mum, and I said he felt there were loving things in this world. He told me crossly though, "You planned it." I said he felt it was my fault it was ending, I planned it, and he felt there was a risk this would ruin the loving things.

In this session, we were able to make explicit between us the fear of cruel hurt that was part of his early world and also part of his present experience of me. In making it explicit, which he feared in itself in case it triggered an outburst from him, I was drawing attention to the world view it embodied. I think I was helped in this by the preceding months and years of sessions in which I had "taken in" his world implicitly and experienced something of the nature of the pain of it, in our relationship. His relief and slowing down in response to my naming the question, "Is this a world where that's how we are together?" showed that he could now step outside it, so that he was less caught up in its stormy emotion. After this conversation:

He revisited the den, wanting me to make it with him. It felt imperious, and tricky. I said I felt he needed me to stay in one place today, but he pulled me quite hard, saying, "I can't do it without you!" I didn't join in, but talked about the fear that he won't be able to do it without me, taking seriously the cruelty implied by the question, how can I know that and still go? From inside the den, he passed me out postage that said, "Wish you happy Thursday." I said maybe part of him wanted me to be happy, but maybe he wondered what I was going to be doing without him on Thursdays after this week—was I happy to be without him? He passed me another note that said "thank you," and I felt touched. Right at the end, he ran out and hid in a familiar place, and when I found him, he said, like a toddler who is loved and can afford to be petulant, "How come you always find me? I wanted to give you a heart attack!" Feeling tender towards him, I said, "Is that what you need to do to get into my heart?" He smiled at me, and I felt that he had a hope that he was already there.

In saying, "I wanted to give you a heart attack!" Dan was showing awareness of his own state of mind. The body language was now translatable, to some extent, into a more widely communicable form. My efforts to take his bodily states and my responses to them as emotional information, as communications about what he was going through, and link it to both then and now when I could, seem to have meant that he had developed a capacity to think of them in this way, and so he could tell me about them, rather than just act them out. Furthermore, he was able now to conceive of a world in which his desire to give me a shock when I could not find him would be received without retaliation—would in fact charm, which it did. It was predicated on his faith in my wish not to lose him—even while he also felt reproachful: "You planned it!" There was no need on this occasion for the cover-up show of earlier times; he could by now communicate resentment openly, verbally. It did not have to be hidden or hurled, as I think he felt it had to be in the days of the shamed "bad baby" with his poo-filled nappy, which nobody wanted to deal with.

In this final stage of the therapy, he was beginning to be aware of and able to comment upon the qualities of our relationship as it happened, so that he was less triggered by aspects of it that reminded him of his early experience. By the time we finished working together he had a developing capacity for emotional regulation, the beginnings of which we had established between us in four hundred hours of psychoanalytic psychotherapy. The sessions were due to end after just over three years because my contract was coming to an end, as we had both long known, but also because he wanted to stop therapy and be an ordinary boy like the others in his class. Had it been possible, I think once weekly sessions for a further year might have been helpful, running alongside the challenges of his daily life at home and in school.

Another fifty hours of the emotional regulation and reflexivity offered by psychoanalytic psychotherapy may have more firmly established these growing capacities in him, especially with adolescence on the horizon. However, as I hope to have shown, over the course of three year thrice-weekly psychoanalytic psychotherapy, he did seem to have been able to make some new connections. These seemed not to replace but to be alongside the old wired-in template, so that other possible ways of understanding experience and of being together were available to him.

In the final chapter of this book, I will consider some of the qualities that may have facilitated this development.

CHAPTER FOUR

Changing minds

In this chapter, I will consider ways of working with disturbed children that take into account what we now know about how children's minds develop. There has never been a more urgent need to do this, on grounds of humanity as well as cost effectiveness. At present there are some quite widely accepted strategies intended to change behaviour that are based on a misapprehension of how minds develop, and so are counterproductive. For example, in a difficult moment with a child, imposing solitary "time out" might be necessary for the adult perhaps, useful in helping them to regain the capacity to process emotion, but in itself it is not likely to be helpful for the child as a way of developing new responses. The naughty step approach is likewise unhelpful for children who have suffered adversity. It leaves them without another body and mind to help process the strong emotion to which their bodies and minds are subject, and so deskills them further. It is likely to evoke shame, which as we have seen is one of the most corrosive emotions. These measures are thus more likely to reinforce than to ameliorate wired-in responses that are adapted to previous circumstances.

Children cannot regulate alone; it is a mutual process, as we have seen from the child development research and neuroscience in the first chapter of the book, to which my experience with Dan bears witness. The disturbed child may themselves turn away or retreat as a de-escalation tactic, like Dan's hiding in the cupboard in the early "Who are you?" session. It may feel calmer than the alternative for the child once triggered, as Dan was by the monster feeling in that session; but even when self-sought, isolation is likely to carry overtones of punishment and shame with its resulting feelings of emptiness—the "dark dead place"—and inauthenticity. Without the idea of someone waiting to reconnect, the child is faced with overwhelming despair and shame. Dan needed me to be outside waiting, and eventually this led to a notion of something more companionable and shared: more regulated.

The same applies to treatment models based on the assumption that the problem behaviour is wilful, a choice, which leaves the child with the desperate feeling we saw in Dan of being the unlovable "bad baby". Where there has been trauma, what is communicated is best understood as a response to perceived threat, which is emotionally and physically present to the child, even though the circumstances that originally induced it may no longer be present. Emanuel (2004) writes of a frightened attacking child patient that:

> The non declarative emotional memory of past traumatic events, including body changes, the draining of facial colour, widening eyes and (presumed) increased heart rate amongst other things, meant that he was again, in the here-and-now, in the presence of a dangerous man. (Emanuel, 2004, p. 75)

In much of the clinical material above, Dan's behaviour was likewise indicative of a physical and emotional response belonging to the past but experienced in the present, triggered by events in the present moment; in his case, often absences and endings.

Developments in understanding of the neurobiology of human development have much to teach us about this process and the implications for working with children who have experienced trauma without another mind to mediate it. One key aspect of this is the intersubjective neurobiology of affect regulation, touched on in earlier chapters of this book, which describes in physiological terms the processes Bion and Winnicott refer to as containment or holding. The significance of this process for thinking about how we can help to effect change for disturbed children is that in maintaining equilibrium through relationship a child can learn from experience. The less he or she has had of physical and psychic holding, the more this will need to be maintained through an external relationship.

When emotional regulation was not available for Dan, his body was triggered into fright/flight responses that bypassed cortical or hippocampal functions that could mediate the response. He had to get out of the room. This was not negotiable for him, and I was mistaken when I behaved as though it was. As I have mentioned, treating it like a choice is likely to have compounded his sense of his own badness. It became apparent that the longer processing route involving the orbitofrontal cortex, seat of emotional connectedness and relationship, could only be accessed in calmer frames of mind—not under threat. When the mind is overwhelmed and regulation does not occur, the more open awareness of the right brain is shut down, and we cannot take in new experience.

This meant that when Dan's body memory was triggered by something in the session, and I clung in my confusion to the tenets of psychoanalytic psychotherapy as I saw them and felt the need to interpret content, this was unhelpful, even possibly harmful for him. Divinio and Moore (2010) point out the role of implicit memory in attachment processes, laying down embodied memories not available to conscious thought. The dominance of the right hemisphere for the first two to three years of life means that infants develop patterns of emotional communication before developing left hemisphere-based language skills later, around the third year. These patterns of emotional communication, set in relationship, cannot be revised by left hemisphere-based interventions, having been wired in largely before the left hemisphere develops. They need moderating by right hemisphere processes. My continuing to talk when Dan urgently needed me not to, in the early sessions I have given above, would thus have meant being experienced by him as someone oppressive and unavailable. On the evidence of the neuroscience, at this stage, the content is largely immaterial; it is the process that matters. It seems to me therefore that what may have been helpful for him in the long run was when he could sense my emotional availability to him, running as an undercurrent beneath the words.

As the therapy with Dan went on, he helped me understand that he needed me to be aware of his physical/emotional state and to act as a processing function to help with regulating it. A capacity for regulation needed to evolve in him, initially through the use of my mind, then between us, and eventually in his mind. He could only bring a thought between the impulse and the action once he had been thought about. Neurologically speaking, his prefrontal cortex could eventually be brought into action to evaluate the stimulus, using past experience of my reflections about what might be happening for him (Pally, 2000). Thus, progress was evident when towards the end of the therapy he hurled things at me from a position on top of the cupboard as he had done many times before, and it felt different—less about rage or fear and more about stuckness. I encouraged him to think with me what might be going on. He answered: "No! This is when you tell me what I'm showing you!" I could not help but smile, and said I thought perhaps he could help me with that now. He did not agree, but he did climb down and stop throwing things, and we did talk about how much he hated me sometimes. This exchange seemed not so much about emotional regulation as about reflexivity, for he was within his own control, self-regulated in being able to answer me thoughtfully though crossly, and climb down. It seems that reflexivity, or the capacity to think about the feeling of what happens (Damasio, 1999), is the sequel to the foundational process of emotional regulation. Here, I was giving the process of reflexivity a nudge because things were feeling meaningless and stuck, but it was there to be nudged, as his observation shows: "This is when you tell me what I'm showing you!"

Another way of putting this is to say that we can only mind about things, or people, when we have been minded about (Balbernie, 2013, personal communication). Hence Dan's "I wanted to give you a heart attack!" towards the end of our work together, which involved "minding" about what was happening between us. However, we only reached that stage after several hundred hours of therapy. It is worth mentioning that three years of thrice-weekly psychotherapy amounts to about two and a half weeks' full-time availability. We tend to think of this as long term. The neuroscience of the process puts into perspective the idea that the task of rewiring a brain, making new connections, could be accomplished in six or even twelve weekly appointments of an hour.

I would like to turn now to a discussion of how these new connections are made. It will involve putting under the microscope some of the elements of the undercurrent running below the words—that is, paying left brain attention to the processes of the right hemisphere.

Attunement, musicality, and emotional regulation:
enhancing neural plasticity

It is evident from the clinical material that Dan's early template, adapted to adversity, was applied to the present moment in therapy sessions, especially but not only early on in the therapy; essentially whenever he felt under threat, which was much of the time. In looking at which qualities of the process of Dan's psychotherapy were helpful in helping him make new connections, one conclusion seems to be that emotional regulation was a vital part of this process, without which no new connections could be made. It will be apparent from the material above that he was only able to achieve a degree of emotional regulation once that function had been undertaken by his therapist for quite some time. As we have seen from the neuroscience, this involves right hemisphere responses to his bodily cues. The whole right hemisphere is involved in mother–infant interaction, and this is where the internal working model of attachment is stored. It cannot be accessed through words in themselves. Schore's (2010, p. 180) work gives us the tools for understanding the implicit processing of the right brain and its subsequent connections into the left brain explicit system. The brain stem, involved in regulation of the autonomic system and arousal and pain systems, connects with the limbic system to do with motivation and emotion, which connects with imagery in the right hemisphere. This is in mutual connection with language in the left hemisphere, but the left hemisphere is not directly connected to the limbic system or to the autonomic arousal systems of the brain stem, but only through the right. Thus the right brain is connected to the whole body, but the left only to the right—taking over, as we have seen, at times of stress.

In writing about clinical practice, Schore suggests that there is a necessary "ongoing paradigm shift from the explicit cognitive to the implicit affective realm … driven by new experimental data on emotional processes and updated clinical models for working with affective systems" (Schore, 2010, p. 182).

Cozolino (2010) describes the psychotherapist as facilitating the rebuilding of the brain. He explains how psychotherapy affects neural network integration and thus brings about behavioural change, and urges a closer look at the neurobiology of psychoanalysis in the interests of more effective therapy. He points out that rather than being a static entity the brain is continually built and rebuilt by experience. Effective psychotherapy is thus a matter of enhancing plasticity in relevant neural circuits. Cozolino's view is that emotional attunement provides the best medium for neural growth and integration. In tuning in to Dan's states of mind and feeling, then, I was unwittingly enhancing the plasticity of his neural circuits—and the converse is likely to be true when I was not sufficiently attuned. The implication is that Dan would be most able to take in new experience when least triggered, and vice versa, which as we have seen was indeed the case. Stuntman and car world were much in evidence after birthdays, with all that they imply for an adopted child with a very troubling start in life. Conversely, when Dan did feel I got the message about his experience of absences, for example, in the "survivor" session, he was able to rescue Ted, to get in touch with some baby "Has and deek" feelings, and to let himself be found.

Alvarez describes the shift in treatment approach towards enhancing neural plasticity, suggesting that "it is not a question of making the unconscious conscious: rather it is a question of restructuring the unconscious itself" (2006, p. 171). Integrating psychoanalysis with a child development perspective, Stern suggests that "without the nonverbal it would be hard to achieve the empathic, participatory and resonating aspects of intersubjectivity", and alerts us to the risk of being "consciously aware of the content or speech while processing the nonverbal out of awareness. With an intersubjectivist perspective a more conscious processing by the analyst of the nonverbal is necessary" (1985, p. 80).

With these warnings about over-attention to the verbal ringing in our ears, I would like to turn to the musicality of speech. It is important to note that not all language skills are based in the left hemisphere. Interestingly, those to do with the musicality of speech are situated in the right hemisphere. McGilchrist points out that many subtle aspects of language such as "pitch, intonation, volume, rhythm and phrasing" are "mediated by regions of the right hemisphere which also mediate the performance and experience of music" (2009, p. 102). Perhaps the "yo-yo" conversations with Dan, arising more from intuition than from theory, may have been more important than I realised. At those moments, I think he found it helpful when my tone was lilting and playful, implying the absence of an insistent agenda and the presence of curiosity that was happy to be led, open to where it would go.

Malloch and Trevarthen (2010) explain the psychobiology of musicality in mother/infant proto-conversation, and indeed the intrinsically musical nature of human interaction. This seems to have profound implications for psychotherapy. I found through experience with Dan that questions of rhythm, timing, tone, lilt, pace, intensity and volume were decisive in making my responses inflammatory, which would trigger an outburst, or regulating, which would facilitate contact between us. Witness to this was his "I like it when you do that!" about my gentle, slowerpaced "CBeebies" tone of voice in the "our town" session. I am sorry to note that I felt I had to spell out the older/younger parts of him in relation to this, and there may be a connection here with his replacement of the pizza idea with karate shortly afterwards. I took this replacement as a comment on his early experience, which possibly it was, but did not also take it in relation to what had happened between us, which I now see as at least as relevant in the shift between motherly attunement and teacherly pointing out and his possible humiliation.

Interestingly, in relation to rhythm and right and left brain processes, Dan would often get the ball out of his box and we would send it to and fro between us when he could not talk and needed regulation. This was not explicitly decided by me or Dan, or negotiated verbally between us. Instead, it developed from a session in the first week when he kicked the ball ferociously at the window, and I caught it and threw it to him more steadily, and a to and fro game emerged, which seemed to settle him. He used the imaginary pot that turned into a volcano in this way too. He loved another kind of proto-conversation that developed between us, involving a drumming rhythm. He would tap on a table or whatever was near, and I would echo his rhythm, and we would build up an increasingly complex call and response, which we both enjoyed, and which seemed to restore his equilibrium and introduce some joie de vivre. In fact, as I mentioned earlier, he joined a drumming group towards the end of the therapy, which seemed to meet the need for emotional expression in a creative way.

It is evident, then, that rhythm in drumming or in rhythmic throwing of the ball to and fro helped regulate Dan and restore a kind of equilibrium when he was unsettled. Early on, this kind of musical resonance was a way of helping him regulate powerful emotional states that might otherwise have meant a breakdown of communication. The timing of this was important, though; I needed to be alert to changes in his facial and bodily expression. Too late was no use at all. Once physically triggered into violent reaction, no throwing to and fro or drumming helped. We had to go through the storm, and try to repair the damage by reconnecting later, usually in a subsequent session, thus helping him to feel that all was not lost.

In saying that rhythmical activities like the football and drumming were to do with regulation, I am not divesting them of symbolic significance. They accrued many and various functions and associations in sessions that I could begin to wonder about verbally as the therapy progressed. Later in the therapy, for example, I could notice out loud that the ball had come out and wonder about what he might need it for. Later still, I could go on to mention that the football often seemed to express a feeling of being kicked around, which he might have liked to take out on me but was directing at the ball. There were ideas, too, about winners and losers and about masculinity that were vividly represented by the football. However, in the foundational stage of the therapeutic relationship, he could not use this kind of reflection. Commenting in this more removed way in the early days, when all the force of feeling was still lodged in his body rather than experienced between the two of us, had the effect of escalating his difficulties in regulation. As the processing capacity of his orbitofrontal cortex developed in and through the therapeutic relationship, though, we could begin to use language to reflect on the process that was happening between us. For example, we could think about his use of drumming near the end to block me out, through fear that I might trigger him and ruin the session. This capacity to think about what was going on seemed to grow out of more right hemisphere-based intuitive resonant attunement, when I could manage it.

It was as if we were going back to the beginning, in part, and building a link between us in baby/mother ways. We developed a motherese call and response, which was not meaningless, but yet was not about semantic meaning; importantly, this was initiated by him. It was complicated because as well as his baby self there was a nine-year-old boy who had lots of other things going on for him alongside this musical to and fro, but his made-up language could sometimes feel like the babbling that babies do. When I did not comment on it but tried to tune in to the sounds of this he loved it, as he showed in his delighted, "You're learning, girl!"

Alvarez (2012) writes about three levels of work in psychoanalytic psychotherapy with children: an explanatory level involving "why-because" explorations, a descriptive level that has to do with the "whatness" of experience, and an intensified vitalising level for children who are out of reach. Perhaps the musicality of emotional regulation belongs to all three, but without it in the foundational stage of a child's life or a disturbed child's therapy it would seem that progress towards thinking about what is going on, and eventually why, cannot be made. This relates to the idea of embodied communication, which is so vital to every part of life that we often forget to mention it. The word implicit means folded in, and the word explicit, unfolded. I think that in my attempts to unfold—explicate—that which was implicit in Dan's communications, I was sometimes working on the premise that if I could only explain what was going on for him, he would no longer need to do it. It takes very little reflection to realise that this approach would not work for me in distressed or frightened moments. The usefulness of such an attempt would lie in how it felt; not so much what the person offering the explanation said, but whether they were able to relate to my feelings while they said it. It is becoming more and more evident that it is the qualities of the communication that carry across from one body to another that make the connection and mediate the emotion, not so much the words themselves. This is not to say that the words do not matter, but the urge to get it right and name things too soon—before they are bodily understood between two people—may have a counterproductive effect. Perhaps this is why the potentially nourishing pizza parlour in the "our town" session turned into somewhere with a karate kick, and he needed a plane and a departures board.

It is evident, then, that how things are said, which belongs to the neurobiology of the right brain, is at least as important as what is said in therapeutic work with children. Again, we know this about our own experience of help in troubled times, and it is implicit in the sensitivity therapists bring to their work, but perhaps it needs to be more explicitly applied to thinking about what helps with troubled children. I think in the "Where were you?" session, Dan was helped to be in touch with the pain of his early experience not just because of the content of the words connecting his experience of me in the room with his early life, but through their tone, pitch, and intensity. In saying that he was furious with me, I gave the word "furious" quite some intensity, and then slackened off slightly in saying that he "was pleased as well" to convey a degree of detachment. I think the remark "I can see what it's like when my stuff is dropped" had a bit of a score-settling tone. A miniature acting out was needed, I felt, to try and represent his feelings more faithfully, and give him a sense of my identification with him, even while I was also the target of the fury and the lesson being taught.

At other times, I think he needed the tone quite light. In the "survivor" session, he seemed to need me to tiptoe up to his lonely plight in saying "the survivor was high up now out of the waves, safer but all alone". This led to his rescue of Ted, and then the risk of falling, which called for a more intense response. There was urgency in my voice when I talked about the shock of nearly falling, and how "this time he wanted me to catch him—there was nothing worse than falling with no one to catch you". It is impossible to convey the extremity of this experience, but I could feel the utter seriousness of it, and as I mentioned earlier, I think something of my sense of him at that time may have been communicated in my tone of voice, for it led to his wish to be found by me as a baby is found by his mother, in the "has and deek" baby hide and seek game. My remark about the survivor really wanting to be found "after all he had been through", evoked by his visible hiding place, was a less intense, light touch way of referring to the pain of his early life. I think he wanted me to know about it, but he did not want us to go there, and so he needed me to be sensitive in dialling up or down the intensity.

Joyful celebratory moments, too, needed careful handling. My "Wow!" response to the dancing waiter could have been underwhelming if too low and quiet, but I was helped in supervision to see that too much might trigger him, too, and that overdoing it could ultimately exacerbate his feelings of inauthenticity. I have mentioned earlier, in writing about the framing relationship, that a feeling of substance is created not so much by the content as by the implicit qualities of the process, especially those of integrity and authenticity. Dan needed an authentic response, but he needed it finely tuned. When I could tune in, and give some musical resonance to his emotional communications, he seemed able to accept parts of himself, as we might say in child psychotherapy terms. Another way of putting this is to say that it seemed to help him bear to be in touch with aspects of his emotional experience that had hitherto been out of reach, isolated, and isolating. On the evidence of the neuroscience, this attunement to his emotional state would enhance his neural plasticity, enabling him to take in new experience—that is, make new connections—through the medium of the therapeutic relationship.

Body language and narrative awareness

When child psychotherapy literature refers to containment, it refers not only to a verbal process but to a feeling process—or rather, to an interaction between the two, a mind/body process. Alvarez (1997), as discussed earlier, has written much about the need for the therapist working with deprived, abused and neglected children to contain, experience and explore difficult feelings that arise in sessions, rather than comment on them too quickly. She uses the language of "projections" and "projective identification" (Klein, 1946) to represent the powerful emotional communications that are felt to be aimed at the therapist by such children—emotions seeking a mind to contain them, in Bion's terms, much as an infant directs emotion at the mother. There are examples of this in the clinical material above, for example, the poo-pizza after the dancing waiter, and the murky waters after he felt I was turning into a monster when I was aware of being left with powerful feelings that were not explicitly addressed in the session. Alvarez explains how "very pressuring projections may include a need to communicate something that may require lengthy containment and exploration in the analyst and should not be shoved back too prematurely at the patient" (1997, p. 755).

This desperate need to communicate something that needs lengthy containment is explicable in terms of neuroscience. Children who have been subject to early trauma, almost by definition without a mind to help regulate and process the emotional fallout, desperately, doubly, need someone to help them process primitive emotion. Their mind has not only had to take the trauma, they have had to take it alone. It is imperative that someone take the force of feeling to help the child's mind begin to make new connections and develop the capacity to begin processing powerful feelings for themselves. The form this processing help needs to take is determined by the child's state of mind, or level of development. As we have seen in the work with Dan, the regulating help he needed, especially but not only early on, was rooted in the musicality and rhythm of right hemisphere-based pre-speech like the "yo-yo" talk. He had an energetic performed vitality, but needed me to tune in to the states of feeling that lay behind the show. I had to do this by first listening to his body language, and then eventually helping him begin to form these felt body states into a coherent narrative, as we saw in the "Where were you?" session, when he told me it was complicated and I did not know what had happened. Getting to know what happened, and being able to bear it between us and reflect upon it, is the long and difficult process I have tried to describe above. It was evidence of his new-grown expectation of such a process that he could demand towards the end: "This is when you tell me what I'm showing you!"

All of Alvarez's (2012) levels of work, ranging from a deep, intensified, vitalising level of reclamation, through something primitive to do with the "whatness" of states of feeling, and then to higher level interpretations involving prefrontal cortex processing, were integral to working with Dan. For example, his early neglect meant that he despaired of being wanted, and did need me to reclaim for him the hopeful feeling that there might be joy in his presence, powerfully expressed after six months in his "You say wow!" At other times, he needed my help with the "whatness" of experience, which he conveyed as confusing and chaotic. He had no way of knowing what he was feeling. The absence of a framing relationship had itself constituted a template for relating, which consisted of frightening, unpredictable, disorganised experience where anything good came to a sudden end and he feared that he himself was a bad baby who had brought this about. Later on in the therapy, what Alvarez calls "why-because" interpretations became possible, drawing attention to patterns of relating that emerged. This involved thinking about the process of relating that was happening in the room, and what it might represent for him—a reflexive attitude, which constitutes Britton's sideways step outside the world of the child's early experience, and is supported by supervision. Dan found it intolerable to begin with, although for the therapist it represents survival and development, and is crucial for progress in the therapy. Technically, then, I needed to move between levels as we explored his internal world and in the process, co-constructed a new one.

I think this co-creation of a new way of being in relation was facilitated by the gradual exploration of his body language states of feeling, transmitted powerfully to me and taken in by me as communications about early experience, evoked now by experience in the room. These needed to find some relation to each other in my mind, which I could then convey to Dan. Each of these aspects seems to have been important: the gradual exploration of states of feeling expressed in body language, implicitly; my reception of them as communication about both early experience and present experience of me and the session; the connections of all three in my mind, and my communication of this to Dan.

Siegel describes "the communication with and about emotion" as having "a profound influence on a wide range of functions, including autobiographical memory and narrative, physiological regulation and interpersonal relatedness" (1999, p. 6). This communicating *about* as well as communicating *with* is evidently crucial. He proposes that neural integration of left hemisphere processes such as "the drive to explain cause-effect relationships" with those dominant in the right hemisphere, such as "the capacity to understand the minds of others" and to be self-aware, creates the capacity for coherent narratives. The clinical evidence demonstrates this integrative process, forging the link between left and right brain capacities. As the therapy continued, Dan was increasingly able to seek and create coherent narratives, a function that was missing or severely disrupted at the start of the therapy.

In the early days of the therapy, by which I mean the first months, as we acclimatised to each other's ways of being, Dan gave me a strong sense of unmentionable things kept out of the picture. For example, he swapped the surveillance police cars for pots and pans, and told me, "the lady can't see it"—the "can't" carrying the feeling of doesn't, but also mustn't. As I have indicated, noticing this out loud was experienced by Dan as objectionable intrusion. I was left with the feeling of two equally bad alternatives: his experience of me as his object was of someone either oblivious or frighteningly aggressive and intrusive, like the vicious saw carried by the helicopter. This was the narrow range of Dan's template of relating, applying not only to his early experience but to his feeling about me in the room now. My contention is that he could not expand his range until someone had tried on that template like a suit and walked around in it for a while to see what it felt like. It was only in this way that I could get to know what it was like for him from the inside, and begin to make connections between his physical/ emotional state, what was happening for him when he was little, what was happening for him now, and, crucially, the relationship between these three. The idea that these are connected, connectable, brings relief from despair "since human beings generally cannot live without explanations" (Bohleber, 2007, p. 339). Taking his or her body language as a communication—assuming that the aim is of being understood— gives a child hope. Without this attitude, these three things: emotional state, past experience and present experience seem utterly separate and potentially meaningless—Bion's "things in themselves" (1962, p. 6). The framing relationship involves a journey from bodily communications towards a shared narrative awareness, including an awareness of the journey itself.

In the new world of the therapeutic relationship that we co-created through our search for meaning, I do not think that his fears about absence and his own survival, or about his badness or that of his object had been removed, but there did seem to be the dawning hope of someone enjoying him and wanting to be with him, not in a compliant performance but in a more lively, love-and-hate, real way. There seemed to be room now for someone to be alongside him—first in his den when he invited me in, and then eventually, I hope, on his journey through life. The clinical material supports this hope. There was a progression from implicit memory of something disturbing, towards a narrative involving danger survived. Stories Dan wrote began, as we have seen, with "postage" of a newspaper report involving our two names, in which, tellingly, the rest of the words were missing, represented by squiggles. The notion of two people together in Dan's internal world, to begin with, implied something criminal and disturbing; headline news, but without the words to explain it, just squiggles. By the end of the second year, he was writing stories, often also crime-related, but in a less chaotic, fragmentary way. In the middle of the third year of therapy, he wrote an illustrated story of a boy and his companion on a series of adventures. The idea of two people together had lost its sense of disturbing wrongness and confusion. Although some of the adventures were scary in places, there was something playful about his account of the journey, and the travellers survived to tell the tale. There was the beginning of the narrative awareness without which life seems meaningless.

Whilst true, though, this account may convey a sense of a smoother progress than we experienced on our journey. Things were often very difficult for both of us in the session room, and the timing of the ending was not of my choosing. Although Dan wanted to stop, or rather, part of him wanted to stop, there were other parts, as we have seen, that feared not being able to cope once therapy ended. I think he was probably on the verge of settling (if settling is a word we can use about Dan) into Alvarez's higher level of work, "explanatory level conditions", which she suggests "involves a capacity for two-tracked thinking/feeling" (2012, p. 4). This capacity seems to grow out of a relationship in which the child's feeling is responsively thought about, and in which the relationship in which this happens can be thought about—the reflexivity that is central to psychoanalytic psychotherapy.

It seems to have been important for Dan's development that the therapeutic relationship began to get to know his early world, in which his template for relating was set. This getting to know happened through tuning into his body language and meant that our relationship could be felt to contain the world of the framing relationship to some extent and not be overwhelmed by it. We were able to feel, and to explicitly acknowledge together by the end, the ways in which he felt I was cruel, and the ways in which I had let him down, without those admissions triggering primitive fears and responses belonging to his early years. His onward progress may be challenged by adolescence, but at the time of writing, I have heard that things are going well, and that his mother describes him as more thoughtful. The emotional regulation and reflexive attitude of three years of intensive psychoanalytic psychotherapy seems to have facilitated the potential to introduce awareness between the impulse and the action: "This is when you tell me what I'm showing you!" I hope our work together has begun to establish in him an internal relationship in which he can reflect on the feeling of what happens, and tell himself, or at least think about what he might be showing the "you" in his mind.

Making connections: worlds within worlds

In Chapter One and elsewhere in this book, I have suggested that the idea of the framing relationship seems key to the question of facilitating change. It applies to how the child was understood and then understands his own being and experience, initially in the context of the mothering relationship and then in the secondary context of the psychotherapeutic relationship. In exploring this question, I have shown through findings from neuroscience and child development studies how minds develop through emotional regulation in an attuned relationship, wiring in neural connections that establish a template for relating. Children's minds are damaged and neural plasticity compromised when this attuned relationship is not available, which furthermore affects their very capacity to take in new experience. This book is aimed at addressing the question of how a child's template for relating, once adapted to adversity, can be helped to develop new connections.

Behind this lies the question I asked in the introduction: how can you change if change happens through emotional regulation in intersubjective relationship and you experience the mechanism of change, the relationship itself, as suspect—even dangerous?

Implicitly relational knowledge stored in the non-verbal domain is currently seen to be at the centre of therapeutic change—not only by psychoanalytic psychotherapy, but by neuroscience (Schore, 2010) and child development research (Stern, 1998). This implicitly relational knowledge, which I have here called the template for relating, has been at the heart of psychoanalytic psychotherapy since its inception, with Freud's (1890a) discovery of the transference onto the therapist of the qualities of the primary relationships in the patient's life.

The studies I have referred to support the view that the process of psychoanalytic psychotherapy, working by the same intersubjective process in which the brain was wired early on, is potentially a mechanism of change for two reasons. The first is that psychotherapy offers an attuned relationship sensitive to emotional regulation, which, as we have seen, is an essential element of change for disturbed children. It seeks to learn the language of the child's early world through taking the child's behaviour and play as embodied communication about that world. This process leads to the possibility of the coherent narrative awareness essential for mental health. The second reason is equally crucial, especially for children whose early lives have been disturbing. It is that the reflexive nature of psychoanalytic psychotherapy offers, possibly uniquely, a context that can address the problem that the very mechanism of change, the relationship, is itself suspect. The transference of the qualities of the child's early world onto the person and room of the therapist is a cornerstone of psychoanalytic theory and practice.

There is an axiom in the world of adoption that "love is not enough". Gerhardt (2004) tells us why love matters, but unless we can also bear to recognise hate and fear when we feel them and allow them into the relationship without retaliation, as psychoanalytic thinkers like Klein, Winnicott, and Bion have long taught, we are leaving out the child's unconscious or episodic memory template for relating, and so are likely to effect no change. Attunement, vital as it is, is not enough. The therapist's reflective rather than (only) reactive response to the emotional communication is crucial.

Bohleber, in writing about trauma, memory and the holocaust, asserts that "the most intensely pathogenic element is abuse by the person whose protection and care is needed" (2007, p. 339). He describes the experiential core of the most severe traumatisations as involving cat-astrophic isolation that is incommunicable. Conversely, I have heard Henia Bryer (2013), a survivor of the torture and horrors of the Nazi camps, talk about how she is able to "put a distance"; to remember the appalling things that happened to her, "but in the background somehow". She attributes her resilience to her mother's strength; her caregiver was not the perpetrator.

For Dan, the caregiver was the perpetrator and unless this was addressed experientially the badly treated dog was felt to be outside the door and little authentic progress could be made. In the clinical material above, I have tried to show how, mainly through physical and emotional communications, Dan took me into his world in which I was experienced as a cruel and neglectful figure who must be placated or escaped from—not only, and not always, but in essence. Unless I found a way to include this essential experience in our relationship, rather than insist on the caregiving nature of the therapy, I think the therapy would have replayed his neglect. Another way of putting this would be to say that the world of the first relationship has to be taken into the world of the second, in the child's experience of the session. In psycho-analytic terms, this is the concept of transference.

Dan needed me to connect his old familiar feelings with his expe-rience of me in the present in ways that he could tolerate, and thus make a link with his past that had different emotional qualities. Attune-ment was the vehicle for the approach to the world of his early years in which he felt there were monsters. It was necessary to first create a new pattern of relating that was attuned, to then bring his early world into awareness in a way that had narrative coherence, and then, vitally, to bring this new relationship into relation with the old world. The danger otherwise is that two or more worlds are felt to coexist in the mind but be out of contact, so that standing in one makes the other unavailable. Dan seemed to find it helpful in one of the final sessions for me not just to feel with him but to tell him that he went to a dark dead place when I didn't come and get him, and he felt I'd been cruel. Earlier in the ther-apy this may have triggered a primitive response, but after over three hundred hours of my attempts at emotional attunement, this reflection seemed to put the feeling between us so that he was not so much on his own with it. He could be connected to it, but at a distance, and in rela-tion to me, so that he was no longer so wholly taken over by it. Making a link between the way he felt in our sessions and the dark dead place of his early childhood seemed to make our world more real and therefore safer by that stage, with the result that he could then come closer to me rather than leave the room.

In a subsequent session, his stance of "I'll hurt you if you don't do what I say" was also reframed in the therapeutic relationship. It belonged to the past, but could also be understood in the world of our relationship now, as not so much a threat as a worry. This connection between different parts of his experience led to an idea of something different. He told me that this was a world about "care—love—cuddles" that he now had with mum. The slow quietness of his voice suggested authenticity in contrast with the sing-song "thank you!" I mentioned from an earlier stage of the work that felt part formulaic and designed to please.

Talking about the framing relationship as a world is a way of emphasising that, instead of showing me a relationship in which one person treats another in a particular way—with scorn, for example, when they are hurt, I felt that Dan was showing me a world in which that way of being was the prevailing order. This seemed to be a fuller formulation of the predicament—altogether a more terrible situation. Nothing outside that frame of reference is felt to exist; all experience is apprehended in that way, and self-protective responses are triggered in response to perceived threat, in the interests of survival. This is life and death stuff. The emotional qualities of the process—the mutual resonance and the musicality of the exchange–are critical here in maintaining or restoring the state of equilibrium in which minds can change. Under threat, people have evolved to react speedily—mindlessly, without the time-consuming business of thinking. My task was to bring Dan's world of threat and counter-threat into the world of our relationship, in which there were different possibilities.

All too often, Dan experienced therapy as a threat, so that he approached sessions with the fear of being triggered into an outburst because of my insistence on naming what I thought was going on, when his capacity to process emotion was not sufficiently developed, and he had strong suspicions about what he was being taken into. There is a delicate balance to be struck here, for not naming whatever is being kept outside the frame of reference can seem to collude with the old pattern of relating. Dan's "No! The lady can't see it!" seemed to be an urgent request not to comment from the sidelines, as it were, but to agree to step into the old frame of reference—the world of his early experience. As I have suggested, it seems to be necessary to live in this world with the child for a while in order to get to know it experientially. This process itself offers a new world view, for the world now contains a figure who is trying to understand what it's like living in this world—although, as we have seen, it will take a good deal of attunement nourishing a growing capacity for reflection before this figure is experienced sometimes as trying to understand rather than as a threat. When such help is offered for long enough, the new framework can experientially contain the old order but is not defined by it. In this new territory, there is space both to visit and then to step outside the old world order and see it from another perspective. Thus, for example, Dan's feeling that one of us, if not obeyed, would hurt the other could be seen differently, as a worry about badness. I do not think suggesting this in the early days would have been transformative; I had to tune into him and feel the hurt and fear first, and it was a long and difficult process. It was only after I had got to know this way of being together a bit with him, that I could ask whether this—our world now—was a world where that was how we are together, and he could say that it was not.

According to the neuroscience, this new territory is made by the process of the therapeutic relationship itself, just as the ways of relating in the early relationship wire in the constellation of connections that constitutes a world map of relating for the young child. I have tried to show how two key aspects of psychoanalytic psychotherapy make this possible: emotional regulation through attunement and reflexivity. Following Siegel (1999), the reflexivity needs to encompass the emotional regulation; the narrative awareness includes the process of relating itself. Wiring in new connections, then, is like making a road as you travel it. Noticing the new road establishes the map in the left brain.

This means that in order to address the problem of relating being experienced as dangerous to Dan, it was necessary to reflect upon the process of relating that we were engaged in, in ways that he could tolerate, and communicate how it felt. That Dan could say, "This is when you tell me what I'm showing you!" suggests that he had internalised a capacity to notice and communicate not just the content but the process of our relationship. He was increasingly aware of the patterns of cause and effect between us—he was showing reflexivity. His question, "How come you always find me?" was another example of a growing capacity for narrative overview of the way things happened between us—in this case, if he got lost, or went to hide, I tried to find him. At the beginning of the therapy, he was not able to take an overview, or see these new patterns of relating. He communicated in bodily ways, which I had to tune into through right hemisphere processes and explore in myself, in the way Alvarez (1997) has described. It was only as we gradually became able not just to feel implicitly but to communicate explicitly about what was happening between us in the moment, thus getting a new perspective on it, that he began to attribute qualities to me and to see patterns of relating, rather than just experience them wordlessly. I suggest that in this way, a new frame of reference, a new template for relating, even a new view of the world and its possibilities, is created.

In summary, what I mean by the framing relationship is not new; but I use the idea to stress the implications for psychotherapy of the way in which implicitly relational knowledge sets a template for relating. Inside this frame of reference, some things are possible, and others are not. If the child is to feel fully taken in, the world of the therapeutic relationship needs to be connected through feeling and eventually through words to the world of the early relationship. Otherwise, we run the risk of leaving something essential outside the room, fostering feelings of inauthenticity and of unacknowledged pain—as in the dancing waiter performance, or stuntman's human sacrifice. Schore (2012) and Dan have both taught me that it is in tuning into the body language that we are taken into the child's early world. In evoking feeling states in me, Dan was giving me a taste of my own medicine, in my representation of the adults in his life. In this way, traumatic early experience finds expression in relation to the therapist, and although it persists it is no longer felt to be all-encompassing. The reframing relationship works through the same process of attentive and attuned emotional regulation that early parenting entails, then gradually builds a mutual connection not only to each other but to the new process as it develops; a reflexive awareness of what happens emotionally between therapist and child. The wisdom of the new neuroscience (Cozolino, 2002) suggests that it is this that helps children with disturbing early lives make new neural connections. Through this process, new ways of seeing develop, opening up the potential for a fuller range of ways of relating, and new experience of the world's possibilities.

REFERENCES

Abraham, K. (1916). The first pregenital stage of the libido. In: D. Bryan & A. Strachey (Trans.), *Selected Papers of Karl Abraham*. London: Hogarth, 1927.

Ainsworth, M. D. S. (1967). *Infancy in Uganda: Infant Care and the Growth of Love*. Baltimore, MD: Johns Hopkins.

Ainsworth, M. D. S., & Bell, S. (1970). Attachment, exploration, and separation: Illustrated by the behavior of one-year-olds in a strange situation. *Child Development, 41(1)*: 49–67.

Alvarez, A. (1993). Making the thought thinkable: On introjection and projection. *Psychoanalytic Inquiry, 13*: 103–122.

Alvarez, A. (1997). Projective identification as a communication: Its grammar in borderline psychotic children. *Psychoanalytic Dialogues: The International Journal of Relational Perspectives, 7(6)*: 753–768.

Alvarez, A. (2004). Finding the wavelength: tools in communication with children with autism. *Journal of Infant Observation, 7(2)*: 91–106.

Alvarez, A. (2006). Some questions concerning states of fragmentation: Unintegration, under-integration, disintegration, and the nature of early integrations. *Journal of Child Psychotherapy, 32(2)*: 158–180.

Alvarez, A. (2012). *The Thinking Heart*. Routledge: Sussex.

Anan, R., & Barnett, D. (1999). Perceived social support mediates between prior attachment and subsequent adjustment: A study of urban African American children. *Developmental Psychology, 35*(5): 1210–1222.

Balbernie, R. (2001). Circuits and circumstances: The neurobiological consequences of early relationship experiences and how they shape later behaviour. *Journal of Child Psychotherapy, 27*(3): 237–255.

Balbernie, R. (2007). The move to intersubjectivity: A clinical and conceptual shift of perspective. *Journal of Child Psychotherapy, 33*(3): 308–324.

Balbernie, R. (2010). Reactive attachment disorder as an evolutionary adaptation. *Attachment and Human Development, 12*(3): 265–281.

Barlow, H. B. (1990). Conditions for versatile learning: Helmholtz's unconscious inference, and the task of perception. *Vision Research, 30*: 1561–1571.

Bartlett, F. (1932). *Remembering: A Study in Experimental and Social Psychology*. Cambridge: Cambridge University.

Bartram, P. (2003). Some oedipal problems in work with adopted children and their parents. *Journal of Child Psychotherapy, 29*(1): 21–36.

Beebe, B., & Lachmann, F. (1988). The contribution of mother–infant mutual influence to the origins of self- and object representations. *Psychoanalytic Psychology, 5*: 305–337.

Berger, J. (1972). *Ways of Seeing*. British Broadcasting Corporation and Penguin: London.

Bick, E. (1964). Notes on infant observation in psycho-analytic training. *International Journal of Psycho-Analysis, 45*: 558–566.

Bion, W. R. (1959). Attacks on linking. *International Journal of Psycho-Analysis, 40*: 308–15.

Bion, W. R. (1962). *Learning from Experience*. London: Heinemann.

Bion, W. R. (1963). *Elements of Psycho-Analysis*. London: Heinemann

Bion, W. R. (1967). *Second Thoughts*. New York: Aronson.

Bion, W. R. (1970). *Attention and Interpretation*. London: Tavistock.

Bion, W. R. (1979). Dawn of Oblivion. In: *A Memoir of the Future*. London: Karnac, 1991.

Blonder, L., Bowers, D., & Heilman, K. (1991). The role of the right hemisphere in emotional communication. *Brain, 114*: 1115–1127.

Bohleber, W. (2007). Remembrance, trauma and collective memory: The battle for memory in psychoanalysis. *The International Journal of Psychoanalysis, 88*(2): 329–352.

Bollas, C. (1999). *The Mystery of Things*. London: Routledge.

Boston, M., & Szur, R. (Eds.) (1983). *Psychotherapy with Severely Deprived Children*. London: Routledge.

Bowlby, J. (1969). *Attachment and Loss. Volume I: Attachment*. New York: Basic.

Bowlby, J. (1980). *Attachment and Loss. Volume III: Loss.* New York: Basic.

Braten, S. (1988). Dialogic mind: The infant and the adult in protoconversation. In: M. E Carvallo (Ed.), *Nature, Cognition and Systems I* (pp. 187–205). Dordrecht: Kluwer Academic.

Braten, S. (2008). Intersubjective enactment by virtue of altercentric participation supported by a mirror system in infant and adult. In: F. Morganti, A. Carassa, G. Riva (Eds.), *Enacting Intersubjectivity: A Cognitive and Social Perspective on the Study of Interactions* (pp. 133–147). Amsterdam: IOS.

Briggs, A. (2002). *Surviving Space: Papers on Infant Observation.* London: Karnac.

Britton, R. (1989). The missing link: Parental sexuality in the Oedipus complex. In: R. Britton, M. Feldman, & E. O'Shaughnessy (Eds.), *The Oedipus Complex Today: Clinical Implications.* London: Karnac.

Cabinet Office (2012). www.gov.uk/social-impact-bonds [last accessed 18 March 2013].

Canham, H. (2006). Children who cannot live in families. In: J. Kenrick, C. Lindsey, & L. Tollemache (Eds.), *Creating New Families: Therapeutic Approaches to Fostering, Adoption, and Kinship Care.* London: Karnac.

Channel 4 (2012). *Derren Brown: Mind Control,* Series 4: Episode 1. www.channel4.com/programmes/derren-brown-mind-control/video/series-4/episode-1/animal-heaven. [last accessed 18 March 2013].

Clarke, S., & Hoggett, P. (2009). *Researching Beneath the Surface: Psycho-Social Research Methods in Practice.* London: Karnac.

Cozolino, L. (2002). *The Neuroscience of Psychotherapy: Building and Rebuilding the Human Brain.* New York: Norton.

Damasio, A. (1999). *The Feeling of What Happens: Body, Emotion and the Making of Consciousness.* London: Heinemann.

Dichter, E. (1964). *Handbook of Consumer Motivations.* New York: McGraw-Hill.

Dimberg, U., & Peterson, M. (2000). Facial reactions to happy and angry facial expressions: evidence for right hemisphere dominance. *Psychophysiology, 37*: 693–696.

Divinio, C., & Moore, M. S. (2010). Integrating neurobiological findings into psychodynamic psychotherapy training and practice. *Psychoanalytic Dialogues, 20*: 1–19.

Eagleman, D. (2011). *Incognito.* Edinburgh: Canongate.

Emanuel, L. (2002). Deprivation x 3: The contribution of organizational dynamics to the "triple deprivation" of looked-after children. *Journal of Child Psychotherapy, 28*(2): 163–179.

Emanuel, R. (2004). Thalamic Fear. *Journal of Child Psychotherapy, 30*(1): 71–87.

Fagan, M. (2011). Relational trauma and its impact on late-adopted children. *Journal of Child Psychotherapy, 37*(2): 129–146.

Fairbairn, W. R. D. (1954). Observations on the Nature of Hysterical States. In: D. E. Scharff, & E. F. Birtles (Eds.), *From Instinct to Self*. New York: Basic.

Field, T., Healy, B., Goldstein, S., Perry, S., Bendall, D., Shanberg, S., et al. (1988). Infants of depressed mothers show "depressed" behavior even with nondepressed adults. *Child Development, 59*(6): 1569–1579.

Fonagy, P., Steele, M. Steele, H., Higgitt, A., & Target, M. (1994). Theory and practice of resilience. *Journal of Child Psychology and Psychiatry, 35*: 231–157.

Fraiberg, S., Adelson, E., & Shapiro, V. (1975). Ghosts in the nursery: A psychoanalytic approach to the problems of impaired infant–mother relationships. *Journal of the American Academy of Child & Adolescent Psychiatry, 14*(3): 387–421.

Freud, S. (1890a). Psychical (or mental) treatment. In: J. Strachey (Ed. & Trans.), *The Standard Edition of the Complete Psychological Works of Sigmund Freud 7* (pp. 283–302). London: Hogarth, 1953.

Freud, S. (1895a). A project for a scientific psychology. In: J. Strachey (Ed. & Trans.), *The Standard Edition of the Complete Psychological Works of Sigmund Freud 1* (pp. 283–397). London: Hogarth, 1953.

Freud, S. (1909b). Analysis of a phobia in a five-year-old boy. In: J. Strachey (Ed. & Trans.), *The Standard Edition of the Complete Psychological Works of Sigmund Freud 10* (pp. 3–149). London: Hogarth, 1953.

Freud, S. (1911). Letter 216, 11th May 1911. In: E. Brabant, E. Falzeder, & P. Giampieri-Deutsch, (Eds.), P. Hoffer (Trans.), *The Correspondence of Sigmund Freud and Sándor Ferenczi, Volume 1: 1908–1914* (pp. 273–274). Cambridge, MA: Harvard University.

Freud, S. (1912e). Recommendations to physicians practising psychoanalysis. In: J. Strachey (Ed. & Trans.), *The Standard Edition of the Complete Psychological Works of Sigmund Freud 12* (pp. 109–120). London: Hogarth, 1953.

Freud, S. (1915d). The unconscious. In: J. Strachey (Ed. & Trans.), *The Standard Edition of the Complete Psychological Works of Sigmund Freud 14* (pp. 161–215). London: Hogarth, 1953.

Freud, S. (1917). Mourning and melancholia. In: J. Strachey (Ed. & Trans.), *The Standard Edition of the Complete Psychological Works of Sigmund Freud 14* (pp. 239–258). London: Hogarth, 1953.

Frost, R. (1916). The road not taken. In: *Mountain Interval*. New York: Holt.

Gerhardt, S. (2004). *Why Love Matters: How Affection Shapes a Baby's Brain*. Sussex: Routledge.

Glass, R. (2008). Psychodynamic psychotherapy and research evidence: Bambi survives Godzilla. *Journal of the American Medical Association, 300*: 1587–1589.

Goodman, S., & Gotlib, I. (1999). Risk for psychopathology in the children of depressed mothers: A developmental model for understanding mechanisms of transmission. *Psychological Review, 106*(3): 458–490.

Gorman, T. J. (1998). Social class and parental attitudes towards education: Resistance and conformity to schooling in the family. *Journal of Contemporary Ethnography, 27*(1): 10–44.

Greenberg, S., & Mitchell, J. (1983). *Object Relations in Psychoanalytic Theory.* Cambridge, MA: Harvard University.

Greene, A. J., Easton, R. D., & LaShell, L. S. R. (2001). Visual-auditory events: Cross-modal perceptual priming and recognition memory. *Consciousness & Cognition, 10*: 425–435.

Harris, P. (1998). Fictional absorption: Emotional response to make-believe. In: S. Braten (Ed.), *Intersubjective Communication and Emotion in Early Ontogeny* (pp. 336–353). Cambridge: Cambridge University.

Hegel, G. W. F. (1807). A. V. Miller. (Trans.). *The Phenomenology of Spirit.* Oxford: Oxford University, 1977.

Henry, G. (1974). Doubly deprived. *Journal of Child Psychotherapy, 3*(4): 15–28.

Hindle, D., & Shulman, G. (Eds.) (2008). *The Emotional Experience of Adoption: A Psychoanalytic Perspective.* London: Routledge.

Hodges, J., Steele, M., Hillman, S., Henderson, K., & Kaniuk, J. (2003). Narratives of maltreated children: Changes in attachment representations over the first year of adoptive placement. *Clinical Child Psychology and Psychiatry, 8*: 351–367.

Hodges, J., Steele, M., Hillman, S., Henderson, K., & Kaniuk, J. (2005). Change and continuity in mental representations of attachment after adoption. In: D. M. Brodzinsky & J. Palacios (Eds.), *Psychological Issues in Adoption.* Westport, CT: Praeger.

Hollway, W. (1989). *Subjectivity and Method in Psychology: Gender, Meaning and Science.* Thousand Oaks, CA: SAGE.

Hollway, W. (2012). Foreword. In: C. Urwin, & J. Sternberg (Eds.), *Infant Observation and Research: Emotional Processes in Everyday Life* (pp. xiv–xv). London: Routledge.

Hopkins, J. (2000). Overcoming a child's resistance to late adoption: How one new attachment can facilitate another. *Journal of Child Psychotherapy, 26*(3): 335–347.

Horvath, A. O. (2005). The therapeutic relationship: Research and theory. *Psychotherapy Research, 15*(1): 3–7.

Hume, D. (1748). *An Enquiry Concerning Human Understanding*. In: T. L. Beauchamp (Ed.), *The Clarendon Edition of the Works of David Hume*. Oxford: Oxford University, 2000.

Iacoboni, M., Molnar-Szakacs, I., Gallese, V., Buccino, G., Mazziotta, J. C., & Rizzolatti, G. (2005). Grasping the intentions of others with one's own mirror neuron system. *Public Library of Science Biology, 3*(3): 529–535.

Jacob, T., & Johnson, S. (1997). Parenting influences on the development of alcohol abuse and dependence. *Alcohol Health & Research World, 21*(3): 204–209.

Johannsen, D. L., Johannsen, N. M., & Specker, B. L. (2006). Influence of parents' eating behaviors and child feeding practices on children's weight status. *Obesity, 14*: 431–439.

Joseph, B. (1978). Different types of anxiety and their handling in the analytic situation. In: E. Spillius, & M. Feldman (Eds.), *Psychic Equilibrium and Psychic Change* (pp. 106–115). London: Routledge, 1989.

Joseph, B. (1989). E. Spillius, & M. Feldman (Eds.), *Psychic Equilibrium and Psychic Change*. London: Routledge.

Klein, M. (1930). The importance of symbol-formation in the development of the ego. In: *The Writings of Melanie Klein, 1: Love, Guilt and Reparation and Other Works, 1921–1945*. London: Hogarth, 1975.

Klein, M. (1935). A contribution to the psychogenesis of manic-depressive states. *International Journal of Psycho-Analysis, 16*: 262–289.

Klein, M. (1940). Mourning and its relation to manic-depressive states. In: *The Writings of Melanie Klein, 1: Love, Guilt and Reparation and Other Works, 1921–1945*. London: Hogarth, 1975.

Klein, M. (1946). Notes on some schizoid mechanisms. In: *The Writings of Melanie Klein, 3: Envy and Gratitude and Other Works, 1946–1963*. London: Hogarth, 1975.

Klein, M. (1952). The origins of transference. In: *The Writings of Melanie Klein, 3: Envy and Gratitude and Other Works, 1946–1963*. London: Hogarth, 1975.

Klein, M. (1957). *Envy and Gratitude: A Study of Unconscious Forces*. New York: Basic.

Klein, M. (1958). On the development of mental functioning. *International Journal of Psycho-Analysis, 39*: 84–90.

Loftus, E., & Palmer, J. (1974). Reconstruction of auto-mobile destruction: An example of the interaction between language and memory. *Journal of Verbal Learning and Verbal Behavior, 13*: 585–589.

Malloch, S., & Trevarthen, C. (Eds.) (2010). *Communicative Musicality: Exploring the Basis of Human Companionship*. Oxford: Oxford University.

Marcel, A. J. (1983). Conscious and unconscious perception: Experiments on visual masking and word recognition. *Cognitive Psychology, 15*(2): 197–237.

Marsoni, A. (2006). Battling with the unlaid ghost: Psychotherapy with a child traumatised in infancy. *Journal of Child Psychotherapy, 32*(3): 312–328.

McGilchrist, I. (2009). *The Master and His Emissary.* New Haven, CT: Yale University.

McGilchrist, I. (2013). *The Right Brain, Left Brain Divide: What is its Relevance to the Task of Psychotherapy?* Confer seminar held on 2 February 2013 at Institute of Physics, London.

McLuhan, M. (1964). *Understanding Media: The Extensions of Man.* New York: Mentor.

Meltzer, D. (1976). Temperature and distance as technical dimensions of interpretation. In: A. Hahn (Ed.), *Sincerity and Other Works: Collected Papers of Donald Meltzer* (pp. 374–387). London: Karnac, 1984.

Merikle, P. M. (1998). Psychological investigations of unconscious perception. *Journal of Consciousness Studies, 5*(1): 5–18.

Midgley, M. (2012). We must find a new way of understanding human beings: Review of the science delusion by Rupert Sheldrake. *Guardian*, 28 January, p. 7. Available at www.guardian.co.uk. [last accessed 18 March 2013].

Music, G. (2010). *Nurturing Natures: Attachment and Children's Emotional, Sociocultural and Brain Development.* London: Psychology.

Ornstein, R. (1997). *The Right Mind: Making Sense of the Hemispheres.* Florida: Harcourt Brace.

Pally, R. (1997). Memory: Brain systems that link past, present and future. *International Journal of Psycho-Analysis, 78*: 1223–1234.

Pally, R. (2000). *The Mind- Brain Relationship.* London: Karnac.

Pelaez-Nogueras, M., Field, T., Cigales, M., Gonzalez, A., & Clasky, S. (1994). Infants of depressed mothers show less depressed behavior with their nursery teachers. *Infant Mental Health Journal, 15*(4): 358–367.

Perry, B. D., Pollard, R. A., Blakley, T. L., Baker, W. L., & Vigilante, D. (1995). Childhood trauma, the neurobiology of adaptation, and use-dependent development of the brain: How states become traits. *Infant Mental Health Journal, 16*: 271–291.

Phillips, A. (1995). *Terrors and Experts.* London: Faber.

Pilditch, J. (1973). *The Silent Salesman: How to Develop Packaging that Sells.* London: Business.

Quamma, J., & Greenberg, M. (1994). Children's experience of life stress: The role of family social support and social problem-solving skills as protective factors. *Journal of Clinical Child Psychology, 23*(3): 295–305.

Ricoeur, P. (1970). *Freud and Philosophy: An Essay on Interpretation.* New Haven: Yale University.

Rizzolatti G., & Craighero L. (2004). The mirror-neuron system. *Annual Review of Neuroscience, 27*: 169–92.

Rustin, M. (2002). Looking in the right place: Complexity theory, psychoanalysis and infant observation. *Infant Observation, 5(1)*: 122–144.

Rustin, M. E. (1999). Multiple families in mind. *Clinical Child Psychology and Psychiatry, 4(1)*: 51–62.

Schimmenti, A. (2012). Unveiling the hidden self: Developmental trauma and pathological shame. *Psychodynamic Practice, 18(2)*: 195–211.

Schore, A. N. (1994). *Affect Regulation and the Origin of the Self: The Neurobiology of Emotional Development.* Mahwah, NJ: Erlbaum.

Schore, A. N. (1998). The experience-dependent maturation of an evaluative system in the cortex. In: K. Pribram (Ed.), *Brain and Values: Is a Biological Science of Values Possible?* (pp. 337–358). Mahwah, NJ: Erlbaum.

Schore, A. N. (2001). Effects of a secure attachment relationship on right brain development, affect regulation, and infant mental health. *Infant Mental Health Journal, 22(1–2)*: 7–66.

Schore, A. N. (2003). *Affect Dysregulation and Disorders of the Self.* New York: Norton.

Schore, A. N. (2009). Right-brain affect regulation: An essential mechanism of development, trauma, dissociation, and psychotherapy. In: D. Fosha, D. Siegel, & M. Solomon (Eds.), *The Healing Power of Emotion: Integrating Relationships, Body and Mind. A Dialogue Among Scientists and Clinicians* (pp. 112–144). New York: Norton.

Schore, A. N. (2010). The right brain implicit self: A central mechanism of the psychotherapy change process. In: J. Petrucelli (Ed.), *Knowing, Not-knowing and Sort-of-Knowing: Psychoanalysis and the Experience of Uncertainty* (pp. 177–202). London: Karnac.

Schore, A. N. (2012). *The Science of the Art of Psychotherapy.* New York: Norton.

Sheldrake, R. (2012). *The Science Delusion: Freeing the Spirit of Enquiry.* London: Hodder.

Siegel, D. J. (1999). *The Developing Mind: Towards a Neurobiology of Interpersonal Experience.* New York: Guilford.

Siegel, D. J. (2001). Towards an interpersonal neurobiology of the developing mind: Attachment relationships, "mindsight", and neural integration. *Infant Mental Health Journal, 22*: 67–94.

Smith, J., & Prior, M. (1995). Temperament and stress resilience in school-age children: A within-families study. *Journal of the American Academy of Child and Adolescent Psychiatry, 34*: 168–179.

Solomon, J., & George, C. (1999). *Attachment Disorganization.* London: Guilford.

Stein, H., Fonagy, P., Ferguson, K. S., & Wisman, M. (2000). Lives in time: An ideographic approach to the study of resilience. *Bulletin of the Menninger Clinic, 64*(2): 281–305.

Steiner, J. (1993). *Psychic Retreats: Pathological Organizations in Psychotic, Neurotic and Borderline Patients*. London: Routledge.

Stern, D. N. (1977). *The First Relationship: Infant and Mother*. Cambridge, MA: Harvard.

Stern, D. N. (1985). *The Interpersonal World of the Infant: A View from Psychoanalysis and Developmental Psychology*. London: Karnac.

Stern, D. N. (1998). Introduction to the paperback edition. In: *The Interpersonal World of the Infant: A View from Psychoanalysis and Developmental Psychology* (pp. 11–39). London: Karnac.

Stern, D. N. (2003). *The Interpersonal World of the Infant: A View from Psychoanalysis and Developmental Psychology* (2nd edn). London: Karnac.

Stern, D. N. (2004). *The Present Moment in Psychotherapy and Everyday Life*. New York: Norton.

Suess, G., Grossman, K., & Sroufe, L. (1992). Effects of infant attachment to mother and father on quality of adaptation in preschool: From dyadic to individual organization of self. *International Journal of Behavioral Development, 15*(1): 43–65.

Symington, J., & Symington, N. (1996). *The Clinical Thinking of Wilfred Bion*. London: Routledge.

Thibodeau, P., & Boroditsky, L. (2011). Metaphors we think with: The role of metaphor in reasoning. *PLOS ONE 6*(2): e16782. *www.plosone.org*. [last accessed 18 May 2013].

Tollemache, L. (2006). Minding the gap: Reconciling the gaps between expectation and reality in work with adoptive families. In: J. Kenrick, C. Lindsey, & L. Tollemache (Eds.), *Creating New Families: Therapeutic Approaches to Fostering, Adoption, and Kinship Care*. London: Karnac.

Trevarthen, C. (1993). The self born in intersubjectivity: An infant communicating. In: U. Neisser, (Ed.), *The Perceived Self: Ecological and Interpersonal Sources of Self-Knowledge* (pp. 121–173). New York: Cambridge University.

Tronick, E., Adamson, L. B., Als, H., & Brazelton, T. B. (1975). *Infant Emotions in Normal and Pertubated Interactions*. Paper presented at the biennial meeting of the Society for Research in Child Development, Denver: CO.

Tschacher, W., Schildt, M., & Sander, K. (2010). Brain connectivity in listening to affective stimuli: A functional Magnetic Resonance Imaging (fMRI) study and implications for psychotherapy. *Psychotherapy Research, 20*(5): 576–588.

Van IJzendoorn, M. (1995). Adult attachment representations, parental responsiveness, and infant attachment: A meta-analysis on the predictive validity of the adult attachment interview. *Psychological Bulletin, 117*: 387–403.

Winnicott, D. W. (1946). Some psychological aspects of juvenile delinquency. In: *Deprivation and Delinquency* (pp. 127–130). London: Tavistock, 1984.

Winnicott, D. W. (1953). Psychosis and child care. *British Journal of Medical Psychology, 26(1)*: 68–74.

Winnicott, D. W. (1956). Primary maternal preoccupation. In: *Through Paediatrics to Psychoanalysis* (pp. 300–305). London: Tavistock, 1958.

Winnicott, D. W. (1960). Ego distortion in terms of true and false self. In: *The Maturational Processes and the Facilitating Environment: Studies in the Theory of Emotional Development* (pp. 140–152). London: Hogarth, 1965.

Winnicott, D. W. (1964). The concept of the false self. In: C. Winnicott, R. Shepherd, & M. Davis (Eds.), *Home is Where We Start From: Essays by a Psychoanalyst*. New York: Norton, 1986.

Woody, J., & Phillips, J. (1995). Freud's "project for a scientific psychology" after 100 years: The unconscious mind in the era of cognitive neuroscience. *Philosophy, Psychiatry, & Psychology, 2(2)*: 123–134.

Wyman, P. A., Cowen, E. L., Work, W. C., Hoyt-Myers, L., Magnus, K. B., & Fagan, D. B. (1999). Caregiving and developmental factors differentiating young at-risk urban children showing resilient versus stress-affected outcomes: A replication and extension. *Child Development, 70(3)*: 645–659.

INDEX

Abraham, K. 62
absence
    extreme nature of fears with 89
    openness together 44
    wild feelings about 85
"actual" object 29–30
Adamson, L. B. 6, 15
Adelson, E. 18
Ainsworth, M. D. S. 17, 30
Als, H. 6, 15
Alvarez, A. 4–5, 24, 49, 72, 110, 112, 115–116, 118, 124
Alvarez, pressuring projections 115
    shift in treatment approach 110
Anan, R. 14

baby language 74
"bad baby" 106
    feeling of 61
    feeling of badness vs. 96
    punishment for 55

shamed 103
badly treated dog 45, 121
Baker, W. L. 20
Balbernie, R. 2, 18, 20, 35, 108
Barlow, H. B. 36
Barnett, D. 14
Bartlett, F. 28
Bartram, P. 47
Beebe, B. 35, 37
being safe, feeling of 53–56
being taken in, feeling of 96–100
    affect intersubjective process 43–44
    child central dilemma and 44
    complexity of 48
    delight and deception in 83
    fears and dangers of 60
    feeling of danger associated with 53
    feeling unable and 44
    fostered and adopted children 44

qualities of space and 50
shame, understanding of 62–63
vulnerability 64, 86
being together 44
Bell, S. 30
Berger, J. 1
beta elements 77
Bick, E. 30, 38, 47
Bion, W. R. 2, 4, 8–12, 14, 16, 38, 77, 80, 96, 106, 115, 118, 120
ideas about dynamic containment 2
theory of the reciprocality of containment 4, 16
bizarre fragments, Bion's 77, 80
Blakley, T. L. 20
Blonder, L. 20
body language
exchange of looks 60
expressing hostility 51
gestures, hand 75
learning 43–103
made-up language and 57
physically demonstration 65
talking or acting symptoms 44
therapeutic relationship 45
transformation to communication 103
Bohleber, W. 117, 120
Bollas, C. 11–12
Boroditsky, L. 32
Boston, M. 3
Bowers, D. 20
Bowlby, J. 19, 30
Braten, S. 14–15, 34, 60
Brazelton, T. B. 6, 15
Briggs, A. 38
Britton, R. 26–27, 39, 116
Britton's sideways step 116
"broken glass" 28
Bryer, Henia 121
Buccino, G. 35

Canham, H. 5
"care—love—cuddles" 122
"CBeebies" feelings 57
"CBeebies" tone of voice 111
changing minds 105–124
attunement, musicality, and emotional regulation 109–114
body language and narrative awareness 115–119
child development research 105
cost effectiveness 105
developments in 106
fright/flight responses 107
hemisphere-based pre-speech 115
sideways step 116
worlds within worlds 119–124
children, with early adversity 72
Clarke, S. 38
communication
of anger 77–79
body language transformed to 103
emotional 88
explicit 89–92
implicit 100
real 89
through hide and seek game 84, 86–89
unconscious-to-unconscious 97
companionable feelings
being together 82
disturbed by internal relationship 83
compassionate response 97, 99
"constraints on ambiguity" 29
Cowen, E. L. 14
Cozolino, L. 109–110, 124
Craighero, L. 35

Damasio, A. 22, 31–32, 108
Dan's psychotherapy
coherent narratives during 117

as ongoing emotional trigger 71–73
first phase of 52–53
intersubjective process in 43–44
missing session of 55–56
physical/emotional state during 107–108
process of 109
"real relationship" in 81
theme of performance in 44–45, 47–48
"dark dead place" 106
Darwin, reframing science 1
delight and deception 83
development of capacity 90
Dichter, E. 31
Dimberg, U. 20
Divinio, C. 107

Eagleman, D. 40
Easton, R. D. 29
Emanuel, L. xvi
Emanuel, R. 7, 106
emotional communication 88
emotional regulation
    capacity for 99–103
    establishing 103
    in relationship 44
    intrinsic mind/bodiness of 72
    Siegel's view on 72
    transformed stormy patterns 99–100
ending
    anger and 69
    explosive quality of 45
    imminent, external disruption of 83
explosive feelings/emotions 73–75
    problem of containment for 75
external disruption, of imminent ending 83

Fagan, D. B. 14
Fagan, M. 66
Fairbairn, W. R. D. 10
fear, sense of, 86–89
feeling of being under surveillance 48
feeling of confusion 46–50, 62
feeling of cruelty 95–96
feeling of danger 44, 53
feeling of frustration 80
Ferguson, K. S. 14
Fonagy, P. 14
Fraiberg, S. 18
framing relationship 1–24
    adult attachment interviews 18
    Bion's (1959) theory of the reciprocality of containment 16
    child development research 14
    complexity of the adopted child's predicament 6
    "core self" 17
    idea of 2
    neuroscience of mind-building 19–24
    psychoanalytic thinking 8–14
    "still face" experiments 6
Freud, S. 1, 3, 8, 11, 31, 36, 97, 120
    project for scientific psychology 36
    reframing science 1
Frost, R. 41
functional Magnetic Resonance Imaging (fMRI)
    scan 36
    technique 35

Gallese, V. 35
George, C. 19
Gerhardt, S. 15, 120
Glass, R. 36
Goodman, S. 16
Gorman, T. J. 14

Gotlib, I. 16
Greenberg, M. 14
Greenberg, S. 10
Greene, A. J. 29
Grossman, K. 14

Harris, P. 15
Hegel, G. W. F. 29
Heilman, K. 20
Henderson, K. 18–19
Henry, G. xvi
Higgitt, A. 14
Hillman, S. 18–19
Hindle, D. 72
hippocampus-frontal index 28
Hodges, J. 18–19
Hoggett, P. 38
Hollway, W. 39–40
Hopkins, J. xii
Horvath, A. O. 12
Hoyt-Myers, L. 14
Hume, D. 35
hurt and abandonment 96–100
    sadness of 98

Iacoboni, M. 35
imaginary worlds, creation of 44–45,
    56–65
implicit feeling, supervision in 81
Infant Observation and Research
    (Urwin & Sternberg) 39

Jackson, Michael 68–69
Jacob, T. 14
Johannsen, D. L. 14
Johannsen, N. M. 14
Johnson, S. 14
Joseph, B. 4, 22

Kaniuk, J. 18–19
Klein, M. xiii, 3, 6–8, 10, 12, 40, 69,
    100, 115, 120

Lachmann, F. 35, 37
LaShell, L. S. R. 29
Loftus, E. 27
"love is not enough", adoption
    axiom 120

Magnus, K. B. 14
Malloch, S. 110
Marcel, A. J. 29
Marsoni, A. 3
Marx reframing science 1
Mazziotta, J. C. 35
McGilchrist, I. 2, 22, 29, 32, 37–38,
    40–41, 43, 110
McLuhan, M. 31
meaning-making 28, 33, 39, 43
Meltzer, D. 49
Merikle, P. M. 29
metaphorical framing 32
Midgley, M. 31
mirror neurons 35
Mitchell, J. 10
Molnar-Szakacs, I. 35
Moore, M. S. 107
"murderator" 94
    extreme cruelty of 95
Music, G. 6, 110

narrative awareness 115, 118, 120, 123
neuroscience 25
    conventional 32
    emotional regulation and 119–120
    framing relationship and 2
    of mind-building 19–24
    relation with psychotherapy 33
    right brain responsive
        attunement 4
    therapeutic relationship and 123
    wisdom 124

Ornstein, R. 20
overwhelming feelings 47–48

Pally, R. 21, 28, 108
Palmer, J. 27
Perry, B. D. 20
Peterson, M. 20
Phillips, A. 37
    model of the analyst 37
Phillips, J. 36–37
Pilditch, J. 31
Pollard, R. A. 20
Prior, M. 14
projections, language of 115
projective identification 115
psychoanalytic psychotherapy 119
psychoanalytic wisdom 19
psychotherapy, adopted child
    being adopted 92
    child's early need 47
    coping with internal world 67–68
    emotional qualities and 45
    emotional regulation 70–73, 103
    escaping from therapy room
        52–53
    explicit communication 89–92
    explosive feelings/emotions
        73–75
    fears and doubts about being
        taken in 43–44
    feeling of confusion 46–50
    feeling of cruel deprivation 93–96
    feeling through colours 87–88
    force of hatred 51–52
    hide and seek game,
        communication through 84,
        86–89
    imaginary worlds, creation of
        44–45, 56–60, 65–70
    implicit acceptance of world 69
    narrative awareness 73
    psychic and physical taking 62
    psychic retreat 67
    "real relationship" and 81
    reflexivity and

symbolic complexity 45
    testing limits 69–70
psychotherapy literature 115
psychotherapy research 25–37
    discussion 32–37
    ideas and assumptions 25–26
    observational approach 37–41
    "raw data" of 26–32
    Wittgenstein's Philosophical
        Investigations 37

Quamma, J. 14

reflexivity
    establishing 103
    psychoanalytic psychotherapy
        and 43
"remarkable thing" 97
Researching Beneath the Surface
    (Clarke & Hoggett) 38
resistance to change, feeling of 44
Ricoeur, P. 36
Rizzolatti, G. 35
Rustin, M. 38–39
Rustin, M. E. 6, 18, 38–39

safe place
    making 73, 82
    reconstructing 75–81
Sander, K. 26
Schildt, M. 26
Schimmenti, A. 62
Schore, A. N. xiii, 2, 20–21, 25, 33–38,
        72, 97, 109, 120, 124
sense of emptiness/missing 96
sense of fairness 50
sense of wariness 77
session material 48, 52
    key themes of 92
    sense of entitlement in 53, 86
Shapiro, V. 18
Sheldrake, R. 31–32

Shulman, G. 72
Siegel, D. J. xiii, 20, 38, 72, 117, 123
Smith, J. 14
Solomon, J. 19
Specker, B. L. 14
Sroufe, L. 14
Steele, H. 14
Steele, M. 14, 18–19
Stein, H. 14
Steiner, J. 67
Stern, D. N. 15, 38, 46, 64, 100, 120
strange situation 30
Suess, G. 14
supervision, in therapy 81
    and implicit feeling 81
    and performance material 47–48
survivor symbol 84–86
Symington, J. 8
Symington, N. 8
Szur, R. 3

Target, M. 14
therapeutic relationship 44–45, 65, 77
    communication of anger in 77–79
    importance of therapist in 67
    late adopted children 66
The Science of the Art of Psychotherapy
    (Schore) 25

The Silent Salesman (Pilditch) 31
The Science Delusion (Sheldrake) 31
Thibodeau, P. 32
threeness 47
Tollemache, L. 5
traumatisations 121
Trevarthen, C. xix, 15, 34, 110
Tronick, E. 6, 15
Tschacher, W. 26
twoness 47–48

unconscious-to-unconscious
    communication 97

Van IJzendoorn, M. 18
Vigilante, D. 20

"whatness" of experience 116
"whatness" of states of feeling 116
Winnicott, D. W. 3, 6, 11–14, 53, 106,
    120
Wisman, M. 14
Woody, J. 36–37
Work, W. C. 14
Wyman, P. A. 14

yo-yo conversations 110
yo-yo talk 115